The All-White World of Children's Books and African American Children's Literature

The All-White World
of Children's Books
and
African American
Children's Literature

edited by Osayimwense Osa

Africa World Press, Inc.
P.O. Box 1892
Trenton, New Jersey 08607

Africa World Press, Inc.

P.O. Box 1892

Trenton, NJ 08607

Book design: Jonathan Gullery

Cover Design: Linda Nickens

Library of Congress Cataloging-in-Publication Data

The all-white world of children's books and African American
    children's literature / edited by Osa Osayimwense
            p.   cm..
        Previously published as a special issue of Journal of African
    children & youth literature, v. 3, 1991/1992.
        Includes bibliographical references (p.   ).
        ISBN 0-86543-477-8 (alk. paper) -- ISBN 0-86543-476-X
        1. Children's literature. American--Afro-American authors--History
    and criticism. 2. Young adult literature, American--Afro-American
    and reading. 4. Afro-American youth--Books and reading. 5. Afro
    -Americans in literature. I. Osayimwense, Osa.
    PS153.N5A399 1995
    810.9'9282--dc20   95-17835
                                                            CIP

This book is composed in Galliard and Nueva

CONTENTS

Acknowledgements

Many thanks to Dr. Dianne Johnson Feelings of the University of South Carolina for her assistance, and encouragement during the preparation of this volume. I am grateful to the following for their enthusiastic support: Dr. Donnarae MacCann of the University of Iowa, Dr. Hugh Keenan of Georgia State University, Dr. Janice Liddell, chairperson of the English Department at Clark Atlanta University and Dr. Ernestine Pickens, Dr. Mary Twining, and Dr. David Dorsey of the same department. I am grateful to Dr. Richard F. Abrahamson who has always been interested in my work in children's literature since my graduate study years at the University of Houston. Finally, I would like to express my profound gratitude to the Attorney, Mr. John Nix, and Mrs. Kemie Nix, Executive Director of Children's Literature for Children and Reader to Reader Africa, Atlanta, Georgia for helping me to have a conducive climate for my scholarly pursuit.

Finally I wish to thank all the contributors for their talent and their belief in this work.

Osayimwense Osa
Atlanta, Georgia

Introduction

The genesis of this book is in the special issue of the *Journal of African Children's and Youth Literature,* Vol III 1991/92 which was devoted to African American Children's Literature. Preparing this special issue of African American Children's Literature was exhilarating. It brought me in touch with some wonderful scholars whose expertise and visions have undoubtedly enriched the content of this volume. From Nancy Larrick's landmark article of 1965 *The All White World of Children's Books* through Johnson's *International Context of African American Children's Literature* is seen a fascinating panorama of African American children's literature from obscurity to limelight. The landmark nature of Nancy Larrick's article is borne out by the various references to it in this collection.

The focus on African American children's literature has been prompted by what I perceived as the cultural link between children's literature of African America and Africa. This focus needs some background information.

In the company of Dr. Hugh Keenan I visited the Wren's Nest home of Joel Chandler Harris the famed author of *The Tales of Uncle Remus* during the summer of 1990. I was at the time engaged in teaching a summer course in African children's literature in the English Department at the Georgia State University in Atlanta. My visit was memorable for two reasons; firstly, I went in the company of a children's literature scholar who has done a lot in scholarly studies on Joel Chandler Harris and I was fortunate to meet two descendants of Joel Chandler Harris himself and to see some of the actual historical artifacts which this master storyteller used. Secondly, the whole atmosphere of Wren's Nest reminded me of storytelling in the old fashioned way — by word of mouth, gestures and total bodily and spiritual involvement by the teller, as well as the listener. It is gratifying to note that Aqbar Imhotep and Cynthia Watts are keeping this tradition alive in their regular storytelling sessions in Wren's Nest. Shortly after this visit *The Tales of Uncle Remus* as retold by Julius Lester was given to me by Ms. Kemie Nix, Founder and Executive Director of Children's Literature for Children, a non-profit organization based in Atlanta. I found it more easily readable than Joel Chandler's original but the spirit in both books is the same. While reading *Black Folktales* by the same author, I found some of the same stories that I used to hear in my childhood days especially in the evening and moonlight gatherings in my hometown, Benin City, Nigeria. There is no indication that Julius Lester went to Africa to collect some of these tales. That they still survive after three hundred years in the African American community is an indication of the strength and resilience of the traditional tales of the African people. At the core of theses tales is a propensity to moralize. This propensity is translated into the printed word.

In March 1991, I got in touch with Dianne Johnson of the University of South Carolina, Columbia, after reading her recent work *Telling Tales - Pedagogy and Promise and of African American Literature for Youth*. I found the work incisive and illuminating. I felt that other viewpoints of other scholars of African American children's literature in a single volume would be a contribution to scholarship in this new exciting field.

Her enthusiastic response was encouraging. Beside her suggestion of scholars who would be interested, I sent out a call for papers to various institutions. Again the prompt and zealous response from some scholars indicates the popularity of the subject.

Undoubtedly, with the evolving human and mental vision and perceptions as reflected in the new tag "African Americans," there would be increasing legitimate demands on the part of scholars to study seriously the literature of the young population of African-Americans.

One just cannot ignore the young population who are the undisputed leaders of tomorrow. And as socializing agents children's books need to be seriously addressed.

From my readings of African American folktales and African American children's literary texts and secondary works like Dianne Johnson's *Telling Tales, The Pedagogy and Promise of African-American Literature for Youth* came to the conclusion that the life and character of the African-American community, its ideals and dreams and its idiosyncrasies and predilections are revealed by its literature. What I found intriguing is that they are quite similar to those of sub-Saharan Africa.

The continuation of African folk tradition in America incited me to embark on a task to bring into one volume reflections of those who have a deep interest in African American children and books about them.

Centuries ago African Americans brought along with them African stories which they shared for their entertainment. The spirit of yarn sharing is still in African American community.

If Joel Chandler Harris had not painstakingly put down the stories he heard slaves narrating on the various plantations, perhaps we would not have had today any idea of how the ancient Africans in the new world relaxed. Certainly there would not have been Julius Lester's retold version of the *Tales of Uncle Remus* as we have it today.

Truly, *The Uncle Remus* stories of Joel Chandler Harris represent the largest single collection of Afro-American folktales ever collected and published. Their place and importance in Afro-American culture is singular and undisputed. (*The Tales of Uncle Remus - The Adventures of Brer Rabbit* as told by Julius Lester, New York: Dial Books, 1987.) In simple bust terms, Harris states his purpose for retelling the Uncle Remus tales: to make the tales accessible again, to be told in the living rooms of condominiums as well as on front porches in the South. It is essentially a keeping of the African oral literature tradition alive in America.

In two pieces, *"My Calling as a Storyteller"* and *"The Piedpiper of Isleford "* are seen two storytellers — Cynthia Watts and Ashley Bryan. I have been fortunate to meet and see these two gifted storytellers in action. Their voices, bodily gestures, and their ability to get their physically present audience involved are reminiscent of African storytelling the old fashioned way.

Some facets of this old fashioned way are found in Madge Gill Willis' *African American Communication Tradition — Oral and Literate*. Willis draws attention in her article to the commonly given excuse that African American children have problem in learning to read because they come from an oral culture. In setting the picture straight, Willis researched a wide range of sources and concluded that "African American children come from a communication tradition that is strong in both the oral sense and literate sense." It is the teacher's duty to keep this in mind and apply accordingly in his or her teaching.

Mary Thompson Williams and Helen Bush Carver's "From Stereotype to Positive Representation" and Frances Foster's "Since the Sixties: Literature for Children by African American Writers and Illustrators" deal with the steady development and growth of African American children's literature.

Where the young child essentially discovers the world of literature is in picture books. Especially for the young child, a good graphic representation of an idea stimulates his budding imagination. As one of the contributors would say, "as milk spills, for instance, in *Two and Too Much* it pours out as a sheet of ribbon. This plastic effect fascinates children with its tactile appearance.

Tom Feelings indicates that the true successful illustration is that which the illustrator produces when he is emotionally and spiritually involved in "Illustration is My Form, The Black Experience, My Story and My Content."

Judith V. Lechner's *Images of African Americans in Picture Books for Children*, points to the traditional bond within the family and within the community which *We Keep a Store* elucidates. But such personal touch within the family and within the community is visibly rocked by contemporary mundane material trappings as reflected in *Clean Your Room Harvey Moon* — games, books, TV, high-tech toys-robots, and too many clothes, spilling out of drawers. In fact, Harvey Moon's room is cluttered. Only his mother's reminders put him on the path to cleaning up. While the title, *We Keep a Store*, indicates communal thrust, the title, *Clean Your Room Harvey Moon*, indicates a command or an imperative to another to put in order what excess materialism has destroyed. Subtly addressed is the need to reduce excess focus on material wealth, and a need to return to traditional values — family and communal ties. This is what *We Keep a Store* and *Clean Your Room Harvey Moon* respectively address.

The contribution of African-American women writers to the development of African-American children's literature forms the core of Rosalie B. Kiah's essay, "African-American Women Writers of Adolescent Literature," which contains an annotated bibliography of a number of adolescent novels.

Donnarae MacCann focuses on the family chronicles of two African-American women writers — Mildred D. Taylor's fiction and Mary E. Mebane's autobiography. MacCann surmises that Taylor and Mebane document a variety of ways in which some modicum of success can occur even under the most difficult and stressful circumstances. Beside content similarities, Taylor and Mebane share a similar style which suggests childhood while still giving enough room and freedom for a deeper treatment of a particular subject.

Joan Nist's contribution in the area of nonfiction, *Master of Nonfiction: James Haskins* is essentially an introduction to James Haskins who is steadily emerging on the African-American children's literature scene.

With the foregoing developments in African-American children's literature, it is worthwhile for achievement or accomplishment to be recognized. Here lies the importance of Lee Bernd's article *The Coretta Scott King Award*. Already an official award of the American Library Association, the Coretta Scott King Award recognizes African-American authors and illustrators whose distinguished books for children and young adults promote an understanding and appreciation of the culture and contribution of all people to the realization of the American dream. Lee Bernd's essay gives a history of the award and mentions the award winners and discusses some of the award winning books. She concludes that readers of every background can come to understand and appreciate African-American culture and contribution through exposure to the books discussed.

The article by Dianne Johnson, "The International Context of African-American Children's Literature" deals with the global significance of African-American children's literature. She specifically draws attention to Lucille Clifton's *All Us Come Cross the Water* (NY: Holt, 1973) which demonstrates that the issues of unity and the diaspora can be explored, even in picture books, without oversimplification to the extent that the ideas become only unrealizable, meaningless ideals. African-American children's literature has come a long way and Dianne Johnson's conclusion of her article is apt:

> African-American children's literature is an international literature not solely by force of definition, but because of the conscious and deliberate visions of a succession of writers and artists who from the emerging stages of this canon saw the world as a small place. Most importantly, they saw the world as a place in which words and images together can help people to be honest about who they are in both a personal and social/political, and thus, international context.

According to one of the contributors, "Children's literature can be born into the world of social institutions that is willing to receive them." More than anything else, the world society of today needs to prepare a generation which should be better than the present one. When Jeller Leppman started the International Youth Library as a collection of children's books from various cultures after World War II, it was not a fleeting fancy of hers. Her major reason was to use children's books as a foundation for international understanding — toward establishing world peace. Undoubtedly African-American children's literature enriches world children's literature, and needs to be studied.

People must know themselves and their culture and use such knowledge as a base to study other cultures of the world. It is on this firm stance that this book offers a window on the world of African-American children and young adults.

— Osayimwense Osa, Ed.D.
Clark Atlanta University
1995

The All-White World of Children's Books

Nancy Larrick, Ph.D.
Former President, International Reading Association

"Why are they always White children?"

The question came from a five-year-old Negro girl who was looking at a picturebook at the Manhattan Nursery School in New York. With a child's uncanny wisdom, she singled out one of the most critical issues in American education today: the almost complete omission of Negroes from books for children. Integration may be the law of the land, but most of the books children see are all white.

Yet in Cleveland, 53 per cent of the children in kindergarten through high school are Negro. In St. Louis, the figure is 56.9 per cent. In the District of Columbia, 70 per cent are Negro. Across the country, 6,340,000 nonwhite children are learning to read and to understand the American way of life in books which either omit them entirely or scarcely mention them. There is no need to elaborate upon the damage much of it irreparable to the Negro child's personality.

But the impact of all-white books upon 39,600,000 white children is probably even worse. Although his light skin makes him one of the world's minorities, the white child learns from his books that he is the kingfish. There seems little chance of

developing the humility so urgently needed for world coopera-
tion, instead of world conflict, as long as our children are
brought up on gentle doses of racism through their books.

For the past ten years, critics have deplored the blatant racial bias
of the textbooks. Last August, Whitney Young, Jr., executive director of the National Urban League, attacked the trade books as well.
In a nationally syndicated column, he berated American trade book
publishers for omitting Negroes from their books for children. As an
example, he singled out a Little Golden Book, entitled *A Visit to the
Zoo*, which pictures New York's Central Park Zoo in realistic detail
except that no dark face is shown. "The entire book-publishing
industry is guilty of this kind of omission," charged Mr. Young.

Are the publishers guilty as charged? To find the answer, I under-
took a survey of more than 5,000 trade books published for children
in 1962, 1963, and 1964. Surely the effect of Little Rock,
Montgomery, and Birmingham could be seen by this time, I rea-
soned.

As a start, I turned to the seventy members of the Children's
Book Council who published trade books for children each of these
three years. Sixty-three of them 90 per cent completed my ques-
tionnaire; many gave anecdotal information as well.

Analysis of the replies and examination of several hundred books
led to the discouraging conclusion that the vast majority of recent
books are as white as the segregated zoo of Golden Press. Of the
5,206 children's trade books launched by the sixty-three publishers
in the three-year period, only 349 include one or more Negroes an
average of 6.7 per cent. Among the four publishers with the largest
lists of children's books, the percentage of books with Negroes is
one-third lower than this average. These four firms (Doubleday,
Franklin Watts, Macmillan, and Harper & Row) published 866 books
in the three-year period, and only 4.2 per cent have a Negro in text
or illustration. Eight publishers produced only all-white books.

Of the books which publishers report as "including one or more
Negroes," many show only one or two dark faces in a crowd. In others, the litho-pencil sketches leave the reader wondering whether a
delicate shadow indicates a racial difference or a case of sunburn. It
would be easy for some of these books to pass as all-white if publishers had not listed them otherwise.

The scarcity of children's books portraying American Negroes is
much greater than the figure of 6.7 per cent would indicate, for
almost 60 per cent of the books with Negroes are placed outside of

continental United States or before World War II, an event as remote to a child as the Boston Tea Party. There are books of African folk tales, reports of the emerging nations of Africa, stories laid in the islands of the Caribbean, biographies of Abraham Lincoln and Jefferson Davis and historical stories about the Underground Railroad. Most of them show a way of life that is far removed from that of the contemporary Negro and may be highly distasteful to him. To the child who has been involved in civil rights demonstrations of Harlem or Detroit, it is small comfort to read of the Negro slave who smilingly served his white master.

Over the three-year period, only four-fifths of one per cent of the children's trade books from the sixty-three publishers tell a story about American Negroes today. Twelve of these forty-four books are the simplest picturebooks, showing Negroes in the illustrations but omitting the word from the text. Examples are *Benjie* by Joan M. Lexau (Dia Press); *Tom's Birds* by Millicent Selsam (Harper & Row); *The Snowy Day* and *Whistle for Willie* by Ezra Jack Keats (Viking).

Those for readers of twelve and up mention the word Negro, and in several the characters tackle critical issues stemming from school integration, neighborhood desegregation, and nonviolent demonstrations. But these books are usually so gentle as to be unreal. There are no cattle prods, no bombings, no reprisals. The white heroine who befriends a Negro in high school enjoys the support of at least one sympathetic parent and an admiring boy friend.

Several books do have outstanding literary merit. Among them are *Roosevelt Grady*, by Louise Shotwell (World) the story of a Negro boy whose parents are migratory workers; *I Marched with Hannibal*, by Hans Baumann (Henry Z. Walck), a boy's report of the brilliant Carthaginian general; *Forever Free: The Story of the Emancipation Proclamation*, by Dorothy Sterling (Doubleday); *The Peoples of Africa*, by Betty Schechter (Houghton Mifflin), a beautifully written report of three phases of the nonviolent revolution as seen in the work of Thoreau, Gandhi, and the American Negro today.

But these notable titles are the exceptions. "Really fine books are still scarce," says Augusta Baker, coordinator of Children's Services in the New York Public Library. Most of the books depicting Negroes are mediocre or worse. More than one-third have received unfavorable reviews or been ignored by the three major reviewing media in the juvenile book field *The Horn Book, School Library Journal* and *Bulletin of the Children's Book Center* of the University of Chicago.

How well do recent children's books depict the Negro? To answer this question I enlisted the help of four Negro librarians who work with children in New York, Chicago, and Baltimore. They rated 149 of the books "excellent" and thirteen "objectionable" in their portrayal of Negroes either through illustration or text.

Among those listed as "objectionable" are three editions of *Little Black Sambo*. Another is *The Lazy Little Zulu*, which a reviewer in *School Library Journal* rated as "Not recommended because it abounds in stereotypes."

The identification of Negro stereotypes in adult fiction is vividly spelled out in the unpublished doctoral dissertation (1963) of Catherine Juanita Starke at Teachers College, Columbia University. By analyzing the work of popular American novelists of the past hundred years from James Fenimore Cooper to James Baldwin and Ralph Ellison Dr. Starke shows how the Negro in fiction has changed from the ridiculous stock character to the emerging individual who is first a human being and second a Negro.

Early novelists called the Negro "gorilla-like," gave him a name that ridiculed his servile status (Emperor, Caesar, or Brutus, for example), and made his dark skin and thick lips the epitome of the ludicrous. The Negro mother was described as uncomely and ungraceful, clothing her stout body in gaudy calico.

Concurrently there were protest novels which showed the "counter stereotype" the Negro of unsurpassed grace and beauty, poetic language, great wisdom, and unfaltering judgment.

In the 1920s *The Saturday Evening Post* was building circulation on the Irvin S. Cobb stories of Jeff, the comic Negro menial. Twenty years later, the *Post* was still doing the same with stories by Octavius Roy Cohen and Glenn Allan, who wrote of Negroes who ridiculed themselves and their race.

Perhaps the public opinion which applauded this kind of adult fiction in the forties was responsible also for the 1946 Caldecott Medal award to *The Rooster Crows: A Book of American Rhymes and Jingles*, illustrated by Maud and Miska Petersham and published by Macmillan. Apparently the librarians who selected this book as "the most distinguished American Picture Book for Children published in the United States" in 1945 were not bothered by four pages showing Negro children with great buniony feet, coal black skin, and bulging eyes (in the distance, a dilapidated cabin with a black, gun-toting, barefoot adult). White children in this book are nothing less than cherubic, with dainty little bare feet or well-made shoes. After eighteen years enough complaints had been received to convince the publisher that the book would be improved by deleting the illustrations of Negro children. In the new edition of *The Rooster Crows* (1964) only white children appear.

The 1964 Caldecott Award went to *The Snowy Day*, written and illustrated by Ezra Jack Keats and published by Viking. The book gives a sympathetic picture of just one child — a small Negro boy. The Negro mother, however, is a huge figure in a gaudy yellow plaid dress, albeit without a red bandanna.

Many children's books which include a Negro show him as a servant or slave, a sharecropper, a migrant worker, or a menial.

On the other hand, a number of books have overtones of the "counter stereotype" observed by Dr. Starkethe Negro who is always good, generous, and smiling in the face of difficulties. The nine-year-old hero of *Roosevelt Grady* is one of these. Cheerfully and efficiently he looks out for the younger children or works alongside his parents in the fields, does well at school when there is a school to go to, never loses his temper, and in the end finds a permanent home for the family. The book won the Nancy Block Award for the Best Intercultural Children's Book for 1963, although it includes no whites except the teacher, the social worker, and the owner of the trailer camp. Only the pictures indicate that the Gradys and their friends are Negroes.

When the Cleveland Board of Education recommended *Roosevelt Grady* for children's reading, a Negro newspaper deplored this choice because one picture shows a work-gang leader grappling with a fat knife-toting Negro who has threatened a young boy. "This is a gross stereotype," was the objection. "But the main story shows beautiful family life among Negroes," was the reply, and *Roosevelt Grady* remains on the Cleveland list.

It is not unusual for critics to disagree as to the effectiveness of the picture of the Negro in a book for children. For example, one of the librarians who helped me, gave *Tolliver* by Florence Means (Houghton Mifflin), a rating of "excellent" for its picture of the Negro. Another criticized it as a modern story set in Fisk University as it was twenty-five years ago. "There has been a revolution down there since then," she wrote. "As a result the book seems somewhat condescending."

Whispering Willows by Elizabeth Hamilton Friermood (Doubleday), also brought mixed response. It tells of the friendship of a white girl who is a high school senior in the class of 1911 and a Negro girl who works as a domestic in a white home. One librarian gave the book top rating. Another objected to the stereotype of the gentle Negro serving-girl who "knows her place."

These divergent opinions point up the dilemma faced by publishers of children's books. As Albert R. Levinthal, president of Golden Press, explains it, "Golden Press has been criticized from both sides... Almost every time we reissue *Little Black Sambo* we receive mail deploring it. When it is not available in our Little Golden Book series, we have had letters asking why we do not keep this classic in print!"

One irate Mississippi mother (white) denounced a Little Golden Book of Mother Goose rhymes in a long letter to the Jackson *Clarion-Ledger*. She was aroused by the old rhymes, "Three babes in a basket/And hardly room for two/And one was yellow and one was black/And one had eyes of blue."

"I bought one of the Little Golden Books entitled *Counting Rhymes*," she wrote. "I was horrified when I was reading to my innocent young child, and behold, on page 15 there was actually the picture of three small children in a basket together... and one was a little Negro! I put my child and the book down and immediately called the owner of the drugstore and told him he would not have any more of my business (I buy a lot of drugs, for I am sick a lot) if he didn't take all the rest of his copies of that book off his shelves."

The illustration shows the Negro baby looking down at a mouse. Determined to get the whole truth about basket integration, the Mississippi mother said she got in touch with the author, presumably Mrs. Goose herself. She said the author gave this explanation of the black child: "He was aware he didn't belong there,, and he was looking down in shame because somebody (a symbol for the outside meddling yankees) has placed him in the same basket with the white child, where he didn't really want to be. Also he was looking down at the mouse as if he recognized some kinship to animals."

It's an amusing story. But the sad fact is that many publishing houses are catering to such mothers of the South and of the North. As one sales manager said, "Why jeopardize sales by putting one or two Negro faces in an illustration?"

Caroline Rubin, editor of Albert Whitman, tells of three books brought out in the 1950s: *Denny's Story*, by Eunice Smith, which shows Negro children in illustrations of classroom activity; *Fun for Chris*, by Blossom Randall, with Negro and white children playing together; Negro and white children playing together; and *Nemo Meets the Emperor*, by Laura Bannon, a true story of Ethiopia. "The books won favorable comment," writes Mrs. Rubin, "but the effect on sales was negative. Customers returned not only these titles but all stock from our company. This meant an appreciable loss and tempered attitudes toward further use of Negro children in illustrations and text."

Jean Poindexter Colby, editor of Hastings House, faced similar opposition in 1959 when she told her salesmen about plans for *A Summer to Share*, by Helen Kay, the story of a Negro child from the city who visits a white family in the country on a Fresh-Air-Fund vacation. "Galleys on the book had been set and art work was in preparation," Mrs. Colby wrote in the April 1965 issue of *Top of the News*, published by the American Library Association. "I told the salesmen present about the book and immediately encountered such opposition that I felt we either had to cancel the book entirely or change the book to an all-white cast. I wrote apologetically to the author and artist, explaining the situation. They were both cooperative and the racial switch was made." *A Summer to Share* came out in 1960 with the Negro child turned into another white one.

Mrs. Colby's experience with *New Boy in School*, by May Justus (1963), was quite different. This is a simple story for second and third graders about a Negro boy who enters an all-white class. "We had a great deal of trouble selling *New Boy in School* in the South," she writes. "Ed Jervis, our southern salesman, reported that one big jobber would neither stock nor sell it. Another one would only fill special orders." But then favorable reviews began to come in from *School Library Journal*, the *New York Times*, the *Chattanooga Times*, the *Savannah News*, the *Raleigh Observer*, and the *Tulsa World*, among others. "Now it is a real best seller!" she reports.

Mrs. Colby is also feeling pressure from those who deplore a story that shows the Negro as a slave, a servant, a railroad porter. "Slavery has been practically taboo for many years now as a subject for children's literature," she writes, "and depicting the Negro as anything but perfect is not welcome either. White children and adults can be bad, but Negroes cannot. So my job has been to tone down or eliminate such people and situations... But when can we lift the shroud from the truth?"

Not all editors speak as frankly as Mrs. Colby. One, who asks to remain anonymous, says it took her two years to get permission to bring out a book about children in a minority group. Another reports a leading children's book club rejected a 1961 book "especially because Southern subscribers would not like the way this heroine tackled the problem of prejudice." Although no other publisher commented on book-club selection, this is undoubtedly an important influence in editorial decisions.

When the directors of eight children's book clubs were questioned about the books they have distributed since September 1962, they listed only a tiny fraction that includes Negroes. Four hard cover books clubs offered 230 books of which only six mention Negroes. Four paperback book clubs distributed 1,345 titles with Negroes included in fifty-three.

Not one of the fourteen Negro books on the ALA list of Notable Children's Books in 1962, 1963, and 1964 won the more lucrative award of book-club selection.

In the two Negro books distributed by the Weekly Reader Children's Book Club *Long Lonesome Train* by Virginia Ormsby (Lippincott), and *Skinny* by Robert Burch (Viking), the Negro characters are Aunt Susan, her son Matt, a fireman, and the handyman, Roman. Richard R. RePass, director of this hard-cover book club, says, "These I would consider neither germane to the plot, nor particularly flattering to our Negro citizens. The main reason why there are not more books with Negro characters among our book club selections is the general dearth of good candidates."

It should be explained that the hard-cover book clubs send the same book to every child while the paperback book clubs ask each member to choose one title from a list of ten to a dozen. Perhaps for this reason the paperback clubs have distributed certain titles which the hard-cover book clubs would not take a chance on. One of these is *Mary Jane* by Dorothy Sterling, published by Doubleday in hard cover and given a two-star rating by *School Library Journal*. It also received the Nancy Bloch Award for 1959. This is the realistic story of a Negro girl who is the first to enter an all-white junior high school that bristles with prejudice.

Mary Jane has not been selected for hard-cover book club distribution. But after several years of deliberation, the Arrow Book Club, one of the paperback clubs, offered *Mary Jane* to its fifth and sixth-grade members. By December 1964, 159,895 copies had been sold. "Only six letters of complaint were received," reports Lilian Moore, Arrow Book Club editor, "all from adults in the South. And many warm comments have come in from the children who read *Mary Jane*."

By March 1965, *Mary Jane* had been published in Swedish, Dutch, Czech, German, and Russian editions. According to *Publishers' Weekly*, the Children's Literature House of Moscow reports 100,000 copies of *Mary Jane* have been printed there and are stirring up "lively interest."

Obviously not all children's books can or should include Negroes. The story of a family in Plymouth Colony or in modern Sweden would be distorted if Negro faces were shown. Certainly no author or artist should be required to follow any formula for integration.

But, consciously or unconsciously, most writers and artists have long been following the formula for pure white books. Some of the distortions caused by this formula are ludicrous. For example, *We Live in the City*, the simple picture-book by Bert Ray (Childrens Press, 1963), tells of Laurie and Gregg looking over the city of Chicago a city that apparently has no Negroes.

Only white people appear in *Your Brain*, by Margaret O. Hyde (McGraw-Hill, 1964). In books of science experiments, it is usually a white hand that holds the thermometer, a white arm reaching for a test tube, white children feeding the guinea pig. In books of poetry it is a white face smiling over the first stanza.

While making a survey of G. P. Putnam's books of the past three years, Putnam's juvenile editor Tom MacPherson came upon an illustrated novel about professional football, with not a single Negro player among the professionals. "That embarrassed us considerably," he wrote.

Several juvenile editors expressed similar concern. "I was surprised," wrote Virginie Fowler, editor of Knopf's Borzoi Books for Young People, "to realize how few books we have on our list that accept an integrated society... as I look at my titles and think of the books (I realize) in many instances they could easily have been books about a Negro child or could have been shared books of child and friend."

Executives at Golden Press analyzed the Little Golden Books of 1962, 1963, and 1964 and decided that thirteen of their all-white books could have included Negroes in a perfectly natural, realistic way. One of these is *A Visit to a Children's Zoo*, cited by Whitney Young, Jr. ("He is certainly right," said the Golden Press editor. "A missed opportunity for a natural handling of the situation.")

In the meantime, the Negro market has expanded to at least $25 billion in consumer purchasing power, according to John H.

Johnson, publisher of *Ebony*. The Negro school population and the number of Negro teachers are growing rapidly, particularly in the large urban centers. With vastly increased funds available through government sources, a huge economic force is building up for integrated schools and integrated reading materials.

Lacking good children's books about Negro history, many school libraries are purchasing the $5.95 adult book, *A Pictorial History of the Negro in America* by Langston Hughes and Milton Meltzer (Crown). Boards of eduction in both New York and Detroit have written and published their own paperback Negro histories for young readers.

The integrated readers produced by the Detroit Board of Education and published in 1964 by Follett for in-school use are now being sold in paperback in the bookstores where parents are reported to be buying eagerly.

The market that most publishers are avoiding is being cultivated by of all corporations the Pepsi-Cola Company, which has produced an excellent LP recording *Adventures of Negro History*. This has been made available to schools through local soft-drink distributors. The first pressing of 10,000 copies was grabbed up almost immediately, according to Russell Harvey, director of Special Market Services. After a year, 100,000 copies had been distributed and a second record is being made. (The first record, filmstrip, and script may be purchased for $5 through the Special Markets Division of Pepsi-Cola, 500 Park Avenue, New York, NY 10022).

What about the children's books coming out in 1965? According to reports from editors, about 9 per cent of their 1965 books will include one or more Negroes. This is 1.5 per cent above the average for 1964.

In addition there will be continuing trend to up-date or reissue earlier books that include Negroes. Among those reissued in the past three years: *My Dog Rinty*, by Ellen Tarry and Marie Hall Ets (Vikings); *Black Fire: A Story of Henri Christophe*, by C. Newcomb (McKay); *Famous Women Singers*, by Ulrich (Dodd, Mead); *The Story of the Negro*, by Arna Bontemps (Knopf); and *The Barred Road*, by Adele DeLeeuw (Macmillan). *Ladder to the Sky*, by Ruth Forbes Chandler (Abelard), which went out of print for several years, has returned in 1965.

This year Doubleday is launching its new Zenith Books, "to explain America's minorities." These books are planned for supplementary reading in high school English and social studies classes. The accompanying Teacher's Manual puts them more definitely with textbooks than with trade books.

Many juvenile editors who state determination to present a completely fair picture of Negroes in our multiracial society add the reservation: "where it seems natural and not forced."

"We don't set about deliberately to do these things," writes Margaret McElderry, editor of children's books at Harcourt, Brace & World, "but take them as they seem natural and right."

"We plan to continue to introduce Negroes where it can be handled in context and illustrations in a normal way." says Margaret E. Braxton, vice president of Garrard Publishing Company. "Artificial books forcing the racial issue are *not* a part of our future plans."

"Most publishers are eagerly looking for manuscripts that deal with integration and the problems faced by Negroes in our country," writes Mrs. Ester K. Meeks, children's book editor of Follett Publishing Company. "If we found twice as many publishable books that include Negroes in a natural and sympathetic manner, we should be happy to publish them." *South Town*, by Lorenz Graham, winner of the Follett Award of 1958, is one of the few books for young people that tells a realistic story of the violence resulting from racial prejudice.

Fabio Coen, editor of Pantheon Books for Children, makes this comment: "A book even remotely discussing racial problems has to deal with the subject with the same spontaneity and honesty that is basically required of any book. To my mind, it is therefore impossible to commission one."

The newly formed Council for Interracial Books for Children operates on the principle that, given encouragement, authors and artists will create good children's books that include nonwhites, and that given the manuscripts, publishers will produce and market them. The Council, sponsored by a group including Benjamin Spock, Ben Shahn, Langston Hughes, Mary Gaver, Alex Rosen, Harold Taylor, Harry Golden, and Sidonie M. Gruenberg, will offer prizes for outstanding manuscripts and will negotiate with editors for their publication.

The crisis that brought the Council into being is described by one of its organizing members, Elinor Sinnette, district school librarian for the Central and East Harlem Area of New York: "Publishers have participated in a cultural lobotomy. It is no accident that Negro history and Negro identification have been forgotten. Our society has contrived to make the American Negro a rootless person. The

Council for Interracial Books for Children has been formed to relieve this situation."

Whether the Council gets many books into print or not, it can accomplish a great deal simply by reminding editors and publishers that what is good for the Ku Klux Klan is not necessarily good for America or for the book business. White supremacy in children's literature will be abolished when authors, editors, publishers, and booksellers decide that they need not submit to bigots.

September 11, 1965
Reprinted by permission of the author. (First published in *Saturday Review of Books,* 1965)

African-Americans in Children's Literature—From Stereotype To Positive Representation

Mary Thompson Williams, Ph.D.
Helen Bush Caver, Ph.D.
Jacksonville State University, Alabama

Good children's literature should authentically depict and interpret children's history, build self-respect and encourage the development of positive values, make children aware of their strengths, and leave them with a sense of hope and direction (Baker, 1967; MacCann & Woodward, 1985; Rollock, 1988). Moreover, the literature should encourage and promote the ideal that every person should respect his or her ethnocultural identity and extend that same respect for cultures of others (Banks & Banks, 1989; Hernandez, 1989; Ramsey & Williams, 1989).

A reflection over several decades of writing and publishing for children gives indications that African Americans have been variously depicted in children's literature. The earliest writings to include African-Americans were the slave narratives such as Solomon Northrup's *Twelve Years a Slave* (1853) and Equiano's *Narratives of the Life of Olaudah Equiano, or Gustavus Vassa* (1789). Equiano's life begins in Africa, continues as he is taken to England (where he learns to read and write), continues as he is sold into slavery to Americans, and ends as he attains his freedom to embark on world exploration, still hindered by prejudices and limitations of color. Northrup was a free man of color but was kidnapped, sold into slavery, and wrote of his experiences after escaping. The perceptions of these two, and of others like them, of the institution of slavery and of the impact of color was different from the perceptions of whites and of free men of color (Edwards, 1985). Both Northrup and Equiano overcame their difficulties by hard work and intelligence. Most children have never heard of their stories. Other slave narratives (Tyler & Murphy, 1974) reveal that glimmers of joy for slaves during early American history were not in books, but rather were in ring plays, kissing games, and made up songs.

Not until the middle 1800s did authors consciously write for children by including many subjects and themes which had and still have appeal to them. This direct appeal to children was in contrast to earlier religious, moralistic and didactic emphases designed for instruction. After 1850, as many more children's books were published, African Americans began to become a part of the printed pages.

Joel Chandler Harris' *Uncle Remus Tales* (1881) were highly stereotypical in language and racial myth. Harris did not interpret the true nature of slaves' use of folktales; rather, he wrote condescendingly by allowing helplessness, not virtue, to triumph (MacCann & Woodward, 1985). Heavy dialect makes the reading of Harris' tales almost impossible. New editions, especially those retold by Julius Lester (1987, 1988), are easier to read but may present other areas of controversy.

Pyrnelle's *Diddie, Dumps, and Tot* (1883), presented good masters and happy slaves in a loyal, kind, and commendable relationship and depicted the African American as a person who knew his or her place. Under no circumstance was an African-American to consider himself or herself equal to his master or to his master's children. This separateness of condition was clearly presented in situations regarding eating practices, the use of toys, and in roles taken in play activities. Mrs. Pyrnelle's other book, *Miss Li'l' Tweety* (1917), continued to depict the life of the plantation as seen prior to the Civil War. In the illustrations in this volume is perhaps the first Aunt Jemima sketch.

Mark Twain, in *The Adventures of Huckleberry Finn* (1884), examined the "peculiar institution" of slavery through the eyes of

Huck, who had to decide on the rightness or wrongness of reporting the runaway slave, Jim. The decision became more difficult as Huck became better acquainted with Jim. Thomas Nelson Page, in *Two Little Confederates* (1888), describes incidents during the Civil War that show the old Negro, Balla, as foolish, and young white children as capable of making better judgments. Page, in *In Ole Virginia* (1887), describes former slaves as loyal to previous masters, but not smart enough to handle their own affairs away from the plantation. Clearly, these white writers were looking back at a time thirty years prior to their writing as one that was pleasant for both slave and free.

Some African-American writers of the same period gave different viewpoints, but these writings were not as readily available then as they are now. Former slaves, William and Ellen Craft, in *Running a Thousand Miles for Freedom* (1860), tell a different picture of the times.

The Crafts' interesting story of escape and subsequent pursuit has been retold by Julius Lester for younger readers in *This Strange New Feeling* (1982), with two other documented stories of the same period, each story illustrating problems of slavery from the point of view of the slave. Lester's *Long Journey Home* (1972) presents several short stories based on documented incidents from the slavery and post-slavery period with African Americans as the focus of the story.

At the turning point of the century (1899) Bannerman's *Little Black Sambo* appeared. Helen Bannerman, an English woman living in India, wrote the book for entertainment of her own children, but many Americans and Englishmen overlooked the Indian setting and saw only an African child as the main character. African-Americans, supposedly, enjoyed this work for lack of something at their level that included a non-white character. An American mother and daughter team, Bertha and Florence Upton, who were residing in England, published a series of twelve books for children, beginning in 1895 and continuing until 1909, whose major character was a golliwog, an extremely stereotyped African doll that accompanied two children on various adventures. *The Adventures of Two Dutch Girls and Golliwog* (1895) was the first of these books. The doll character, the Golliwog, was produced as a doll in England into the 1960s when groups objecting to the stereotype succeeded in ending its manufacture. Bertha Upton's original doll, from which others were made, is housed at Checkers, the home of the British Prime Minister.

Eneas Africanus (1920) is a typical example of white writers' images of African-Americans in the first quarter of the 20th century. Eneas is to deliver a silver cup to Tommeyville, a near-by place that he never reaches; and in his ignorance of geography, he goes in the opposite direction. The author describes him as faithful, and so he is. He delivers the cup eight years and after more than 3000 miles of wandering. Lofting's *The Voyages of Dr. Dolittle* (1922) projects the only African character, Bumpo, as a former student at Oxford who leaves the university because he must wear shoes. Bumpo is seen as ridiculous because of his inappropriate use of big words and his naive behavior. Maud Lindsay uses the African-American stereotype of "uncle or aunty" with the use of dialect and stupidity in *Little Missy* (1922).

Several authors, both black and white, wrote using dialect during the 1930s because these manuscripts could get published. Weaver introduced *Frawg* (1930), where the principal human character bears this distorted pronunciation of the animal name. Frawg's major preoccupation is with the eating of watermelons and in conversing with his dog, who is far superior in intelligence than Frawg. The illustrations are typical stereotypes — large lips, bug eyes, bare-footed, and watermelons. Braune's *Honey Chile* (1937) continued by language and illustration the stereotypes of plantation life, and Credle's *Across the Cotton Patch* (1935) depicted twin girls with names that are not commonly used among humans, Atlantic and Pacific, and their baby sister, Magnolia Blossom. Credle also used the terms "culled boys" and "yaller gals" as spoken by the African American children, possible only if white writers were choosing the words. Maud and Miska Petersham, award winning authors and illustrators, used illustrations of African-Americans in two non-fiction children's book, *The Story of Sugar* (1936) and *The Story Book of Cotton* (1939). In both of these books, African-American characters, especially children, are shown bare-foot working in fields or playing around bales of cotton or clumps of sugarcane.

Some interesting breakthroughs took place in the 1930s. Eva Knox Evans, in her books about Araminta (*Araminta*, 1930; *Araminta's Goat*, 1938) presented stories with all African-American characters. Erick Berry, illustrator of these books, presented pleasing children, even if there were piles of watermelons. Araminta is a little girl who visits her grandmother in the country where she learns how people dealt with routine activities, such as getting water, in a different way from people in the city. Florence Crannell Means, in *Shuttered Windows* (1938), used all African-American characters presented realistically with strong character portraits by Armstrong Sperry. Again, Stella Sharpe in *Tobe* (1939) used all African Americans with photographs to depict ordinary happenings of a typical farm family in South Carolina. In all of these, good family relationships were presented, including the presence of a father.

The early 1940s reflected the same patterns of the 1930s . Inez Hogan produced several books, *Nicodemus Laughs* (1940), *Nicodemus Runs Away* (1942), and *Nicodemus and the Goose* (1945), along with her 1939 *Mule Twins*, that depicted African-American children as stupid, funloving, barefooted, and with mothers who wore checkered or polka-dot dresses and with large white aprons and headwraps. These books were reprinted several times through 1955 producing a distorted image for African American children to see themselves. Although Arna Bontemps' *Golden Slippers, an Anthology of Negro Poetry for Young Readers* (1941) added a welcome item for black children, Henrietta Sharon's illustrations did nothing to enhance the image of African-American children. Noteworthy during the 1940s was *Two is a Team* (1945), an effort at integration in picture books where an African-American boy and a white boy learn to cooperate and play with scooters. Florence Hayes, in *Skid* (1948), and Jesse Jackson, in *Call me Charley* (1945), illustrated an altered mind set about integration following the end of World War II. Each book was an attempt to place an African-American child in an all white community (school) and have the child succeed because of athletic ability and adaptation to middle class white patterns. Ellen Tarry's *My Dog Rinty* (1946), depicts African-Americans in a positive family manner as the story is told about a boy and his dog. The theme is universal with black and white photographic illustrations similar to *Tobe*.

One most unusual book for the time was Eva Knox Evans' *All About Us* (1947). This was a non-fiction effort to reduce prejudice in several areas, not just for African-Americans. Albert Einstein's statement in the beginning of the book commends the book's efforts at promoting ethnic likenesses rather than ethnic differences. The illustration on blood types is quite interesting indicating that various ethnic groups can have the same blood types. Another important book was Meadowcraft's *By Secret Railway* (1948). In this book it is another African-American family who assists slaves who have just left the south instead of having to rely upon assistance from white Americans.

The 1950s inaugurated a period of biography and fictionalized biography. Arna Bontemps produced Chariot in the Sky, a Story of the Jubilee Singers (1951), a story about students at Fisk University, who had been former slaves, and then made up the group known as the Jubilee Singers. In 1871 this group toured Europe and the United States. The writing was commendable, but the illustrations continued the previous stereotypes. Many biographies of George Washington Carver appeared, including one by Bontemps, The Story of George Washington Carver (1954). Florence Crannell Means wrote Carver's George, a Biography of George Washington Carver (1952). The turbulent fifties was a time when writers chose carefully the subjects of their biographies. There were few "living" African-Americans presented in books. Bontemps wandered into a more controversial area in the biography of Frederick Douglass (1959). It is always interesting to see how Douglass' second marriage is handled by biographers. Bontemps states that a second marriage took place, but fails to mention that the second wife was white. Dorothy Sterling chose Captain for the Planter the Story of Robert Smalls (1958). Sterling's book recounted the life of Smalls, who was born a slave, learned seafaring, became a captain, and was later elected to Congress after the Civil War. Amos Fortune. Free Man (Yates, 1950), was a fictionalized biography of an African-American that won the Newbery Award, but MacCann (1985) in discussing the book says that the author's descriptions are condescending and make the African appear almost sub-human upon his arrival in America. He was sold into slavery, but he managed to work hard, earn money, and buy his own freedom.

Two books of fiction were significant. Dorothy Sterling entered the desegregation/integration theme with *Mary Jane* (1959). Reflecting the feelings of some people of the time was *Little Vic* (Gates, 1951), where a physical attack was made upon an African-American child because of his color. The 50s were turbulent times.

There was a remarkable change in books during the 1960s when Ezra Jack Keats (1962) began writing and illustrating African-Americans in a more positive way through his creation of *The Snowy Day* (1962). This book depicts a boy in a real home-life situation who encounters an experience which is universal to any ethnic group. Keats' books were welcome additions to the publishing world of children's literature. No mention was made in the text of Peter's race, but the illustrations were clearly African-American. The illustrations were, for the most part, non-stereotyped. He followed *The Snowy*

Day with *Peter's Chair* (1967) continuing the story of Peter and this time presented an entire family instead of just a mother and son. *Goggles!* (1969) showed more of the inner city neighborhood with inner city problems. *A Letter to Amy* (1968) took Peter into the early problems of friendship between boys and girls. In all of these the idea of ethnicity is not mentioned in the text, but is apparent only in the authentic and generally pleasing illustrations. Keats, who was white, did let his own background knowledge of stereotypes sometimes come through in his illustrations, such as size and clothing of female African-Americans.

Other writers and illustrators were entering the picture book field. Elizabeth Hill's *Evan's Corner* (1967), illustrated by Nancy Grossman, showed the problems of urban housing when eight family members must share a two-room apartment. Each can have a corner. The text does not mention racial make-up of the family, but the illustrations are non-stereotyped African-Americans. Ann Scott's *Sam* (1967) is well illustrated by Symeon Shimin. Sam, a child who is learning to find his place within the family, is a character worthy of knowing. John Steptoe's *Stevie* (1969), written and illustrated by a seventeen-year-old African-American, dealt with family care problems and sharing. The text uses some dialect but in an acceptable manner, and the illustrations realistically depict a modern African-American apartment.

Biographies, such as Aliki's *A Weed is a Flower: The Life of George Washington Carver* (1965) began to tell history as it was including actual facts which were not always pleasant. Sam and Beryl Epstein did yet another biography of *George Washington Carver. Negro Scientist* (1961) for children as young as second grade. Dorothy Sterling selected *Lucretia Mott. Gentle Warrior* (1964) to add a much needed biography of a female African-American. Esther Douty detailed the life of the free man of color as successful businessman in *Forten the Sailmaker, Pioneer Champion of Negro Rights* (1968), and Ellen Tarry reached into more recent times for *Young Jim. the Early Years of James Weldon Johnson* (1967). Carver, Mott, Forten, and Johnson are African-Americans that children should know about in American history. Harold Felton added the flavor of the west in his biographies of *Jim Beckworth, Negro Mountain Man* (1966), *Nat Love. Negro Cowboy* (1969), and *Edward Rose. Negro Trail Blazer* (1967). Writers today do not feel it necessary to identify by race the subject of their biography in the title. In the sixties, there was much demand for such material because of the Elementary and Secondary

Education Act that provided funds for libraries to update holdings.

Fiction for older children received much attention in the sixties. Virginia Hamilton's *Zeely* (1967), with illustrations by Symeon Shimin, provided upper elementary African-American girls with an interesting positive image. Hamilton followed with *The House of Dies Drear* (1968), a contemporary realistic mystery involving a house that was used in the days of the Underground Railroad. She included much history and noted the resourcefulness of African-Americans in solving their own problems. Kristin Hunter's *The Soul Brothers and Sister Lou* (1968) used a fourteen-year-old girl protagonist in illustrating both urban poverty and the use of musical talent to accomplish one's goals. *Sounder* (1969) by William Armstrong used an African-American family of the turn of the century as subject matter, but many African Americans objected to the stereotyped helplessness of the characters who were further demeaned by having no name. *Mississippi Possum* (1965), by Miska Miles, had the possum as the main character fleeing from a flood. The family following his trail was African-American. The story is well-written and the illustrations are positive.

Other non-fiction materials produced in the sixties involved folktales, poetry, and books that emphasized African-American heritage. African folktales were presented in Verna Aardema's *Tales from the Story Hat* (1960), Arkhurst's *The Adventures of Spider* (1964), and Hamilton's *Time-Ago Tales of Jahdu* (1969). Arna Bontemps selected poetry for *American Negro Poetry* (1963) primarily from the writers of the Harlem Renaissance and Arnold Adoff's *I Am the Darker Brother: An Anthology of Modern Poems by Black Americans* (1970) relied on more recent poets. Two books that were important in establishing African-American heritage were Lester's *To Be A Slave* (1968) and McGovern's *Black is Beautiful* (1969). McGovern's book is appropriate for younger children in that many beautiful things, not just people, are pictured in photographs.

Virginia Hamilton wrote extensively in the 1970s of the African-American experience. Some of these works are *M.C. Higgins, the Great* (1974), a many layered look at life in African American Appalachia; *The Planet of Junior Brown* (1971), a disturbing book about problems in adapting American education to diverse students and lifestyles; and two biographies, *Paul Robeson: The Life and Times of a Free Man* (1974) and *W. E. B. DuBois* (1972). Both biographical subjects were controversial African-Americans for their stands on political issues.

Lucille Clifton wrote especially for the younger reader. *Don't You Remember?* (1972) concerns a four-year old and her birthday, *The Boy Who Didn't Believe in Spring* (1973) has pictures with an interracial friendship, but the problem lies in the boy's insisting on proof of spring! Several of Clifton's stories are about Everett Anderson, a small African-American child trying to find himself in his world. *Everett Anderson's Friend* (1976) and *Everett Anderson's Nine Month Long* (1978) indicate the usual family situations involving children, but African-American children can see themselves in these situations rather than having to translate stories with white characters. Clifton's *Amifika* (1977) reveals the thoughts and concerns of a young boy whose father is coming home after a period of being away, and the child questions whether the father will remember him. Clifton also addresses African American heritage in *The Lucky Stone* (1979) as a great grandmother relates to her great-granddaughter the fortunes of a stone as it passed from those born in slavery to those in the present generation.

Other African American writers emerged during the period of the 70s. Sharon Bell Mathis' *The Hundred Penny Box* (1975), illustrated by Leo and Diane Dillon, drew a picture of modern urban family life involving intergenerational conflicts wherein a young African American boy was the major facilitator. Mathis' *A Teacup Full of Roses* (1972) and *Listen to the Fig Tree* (1974) both dealt with intense problems generally found by older children — alcoholism, child abuse, blindness, and despair. The characters are non-stereotyped, but the situations may be realistically drawn as to create a feeling of helplessness in a non-caring society. Eloise Greenfield in *Sister* (1974) and in *Talk About a Family* (1978) depicts family strength wherein each family member works to solve problems, and Brenda Wilkinson's *Ludell* (1975) recounts the strengths of a poor African-American family in the 1950s who struggle to obtain the bare necessities and a TV.

Walter Dean Myers' *It Ain't All for Nothin'* (1975) continues to present the murky side of inner city life where children must bear grown-up responsibilities such as taking care of parents or grandparents who are incapable of taking care of themselves. Some children do live this way. Perhaps seeing a similar situation in a book will let them know that they are not alone and that there is hope.

Bette Green, a white author, wrote *Philip Likes Me. I Reckon Maybe* (1974) that filled a need for humor, for ideas on boy-girl relationships at a younger age, and for coping with school. This book may be used from grades 3 to 8 as it has no stereotypes, good illustrations, and language that is acceptable for all ages.

Books of poetry were numerous. June Jordan's *The Voice of the Children* (1970) used poetry from African American children about their feelings. Arnold Adoff's *My Black Me A Beginning Book of Black Poetry* (1974) and *Black is Brown is Tan* (1973), Tom Feelings and Niki Grimes' *Something on My Mind* (1978), and Eloise Greenfield's *Honey. I Love and Other Love Poems* (1972) made major contributions to African-American children's poetry. Biography for younger readers (grades 2 through 4) appeared with civil rights leaders as subject matter. Examples are Adoff's *Malcolm X* (1970), June Jordan's *Fannie Lou Hamer* (1972), Louise Meriwether's *Don't Ride the Bus on Monday. the Rosa Parks Story* (1973), and Ruby Radford's *Mary McLeod Bethune* (1973). Biographies for older children were also evident. Fisher's *Picture Book of Revolutionary War Heroes* (1970) included, but was not limited to, African-Americans. Lester's *Long Journey Home. Stories from Black History* (1972) was based on documented sources. *Sojourner Truth. a Self-Made Woman* (1974) by Victoria Ortiz and Katz' *Black People Who Made the West (1977)* placed the lives of these people in historical perspective.

Picture books of the 70s became quite beautiful. Feelings' *Moja Means One, A Swahili Cunting Book* (1971), and *Jumbo Means Hello, a Swahili Alphabet Book* (1974) allowed Feelings to depict African children for African-American children to see. The techniques involved produced a luminous and happy group of children. Feelings' *Black Pilgrimage* (1972) let Feelings interpret modern African-American children in a non-stereotyped way. Ezra Jack Keats' *Apt. 3* (1971) provided a contrast in color and collage to the works of Feelings. Thomas' *Lordy, Aunt Hattie* (1973) with illustrations by Thomas di Grazie, used vivid full page watercolors of a happy African-American girl spending her summer in the country. G. Gray's *Sned Wendell* (1974) has drawings by Symeon Shimin that portray warmth and happiness on an oversize page. Leo and Diane Dillon's illustrations in *The Hundred Penny Boy* (Mathis, 1975), in Aardema's *Why Mosquitoes Buzz in People's Ears* (1975), and in Musgrove's *Ashanti to Zulu, African Traditions* (1976) were award winning tributes to non-stereotyped representations.

The decade of the 1980s produced a rich variety in stories and picture books featuring the African-American child and the young African-American adult. Lucille Clifton continued to write about ordinary situations affecting all children as in *My Friend Jacob* (1980) which featured the friendship between a retarded older child and a non-retarded African-American younger child, and in *Everett Anderson's Goodbye* (1983) which dealt with the problem of the death of the father and the stages of grief encountered by the child. Eloise Greenfield's words and Floyd Cooper's illustrations in *Grandpa's Face* (1988) present the modern working grandfather (an actor) in a sympathetic, interesting study of relationships. Patricia McKissack presented an African-American child in a humorous positive way in *Flossie and the Fox* (1986), a different and witty version of Little Red Riding Hood. Rachel Isadora's illustrations show an independent, lively young girl with features not unlike those used by Erick Berry in the Araminta books. McKissack went to her own background to write *Mirandy and Brother Wind* (1988) a tale of two youngsters and their first cakewalk. The illustrations by Jerry Pinkney give highly positive images of life of African-Americans in the early 20th century with scenes of their homes, their dress, their quilts, their chores, and their pastimes. Pinkney also illustrated San Souci's *The Talking Eggs* (1989) with similar pictures to relate the Creole folktale from Louisiana. The rich watercolors reflect life and energy in the happy and expressive faces of the characters in a non-stereotyped manner. Another book illustrated by Jerry Pinkney is Flournoy's *The Patchwork Quilt* (1985) where scraps from family clothing are used to relate family stories. As usual, the illustrations, especially of the quilt, are outstanding. John Steptoe, in *Daddy is a Monster...Sometimes* (1980) dealt with children's perception of adults when the child must be disciplined, and in *Mufaro's Beautiful Daughters. an African Tale* (1987), Steptoe presented in stunning pictures the ruins from an ancient city in Zimbabwe and African girls in non-stereotyped, sympathetic portraits. Alan Schroeder in *Ragtime Tumpie* (1989) did a fictionalized biography of Josephine Baker for very young readers with illustrations by Bernie Fuchs. The story and the full page, full color illustrations seem to give movement in themselves as a young girl begins to know that she must dance. Good family relationships, along with the art of storytelling, are shown in *Tell Me a Story. Mama* (1989) by Angela Johnson and illustrated by David Soman. Mary Stolz' *Storm in the Night* (1988), illustrated by Pat Cummings, uses the setting of a storm for a grandfather to tell of his boyhood to a grandson. The illustrations reflect the foreboding of the storm and the serenity of the calm following the storm. Joyce Barrett's *Willie's not the Hugging Kind* (1989) shows a young school-age boy who wishes to be left alone, especially not be hugged by everyone he meets. The illustrations indicate a child who may be frightened by persons he does not know. He later relents and agrees some hugs are acceptable. Ann Cameron introduced Julian in *The Stories Julian Tells* (1981) as a seven-year-old African-American who gets into and out of trouble with his brother, his friends, and himself. He is a delightful character for other seven-years-old to enjoy.

Walter Dean Myers and Virginia Hamilton wrote books for older children dealing with various problems. Myers' books for middle grade students *The Mouse Rap* (1990), *Me, Mop, and the Moondance Kids* (1988), and *Scorpions* (1988) have believable characters in non-stereotyped roles encountering mystery, searching for family, and staying alive amid gangs and guns. His books for older readers *Won't Know Till I Get There* (1982) and *Fallen Angels* (1988) address the problems of intergenerational togetherness and Vietnam. These are strong ideas for older readers with some unsavory language and life conditions. Virginia Hamilton wrote numerous books for maturing children. *Anthony Burns: the Defeat and Triumph of a Fugitive Slave* (1988) returns to a theme of African-American use of wits and abilities to achieve a goal. *Sweet Whispers, Brother Rush* (1982) delves into the mystic and the real in a somewhat disturbing picture of unusual family life. Hamilton departed from novels and biographies in *In the Beginning* (1988) which was a book of non-fiction tales of creation from many sources, not just African-American. *The People Could Fly: American Black Folktales* (1985) was a collection of stories of the supernatural and other slave tales. *The Bells of Christmas* (1989) depicts an 1890 Christmas as celebrated by an African-American family in Ohio with wooden bathtubs, woodburning stoves, and a fairly surprising middle class atmosphere. Hamilton drew from her own family's background to show this holiday in a different light.

Although Brian Lanker did not write and photograph *I Dream a World* (1989) for children's literature, elementary children, especially girls, should have this book available. Seventy-five portraits of African American black women who have changed their world and time are placed next to interviews with these women. It is indeed a tribute to the women and a model for those yet to come.

As we enter the 1990s and beyond, the images of African-Americans in children's literature have certainly improved over time, yet some stereotypes persist. Mary Warwick's *Alabama Angels* (1989) published by Blackbelt Press, an African-American press, has several angels floating through its pages all looking exactly alike with no distinguishing features and hardly any features at all. These are surrounded by fields of cotton. Compare this book with that of Hale's *Mary Had a Little Lamb* (1990) where the traditional rhyme is illustrated with full page color photographs of a middle-class African American girl of about seven years of age. Also compare with Crescent Dragonwagon's *Homeplace* (1990), illustrated by Jerry Pinkney, where the ruins of an old house are explored by several people of various ethnic groups who recall the previous occupants of the house who were also from various ethnic backgrounds. Pinkney's watercolor illustrations cast a misty mystery about the story of the old house. There may be fewer books published centered about African-Americans, but the quality of writing and illustration is providing better mirrors from which African-American children can find themselves.

CHILDREN'S BOOKS NOTED IN TEXT

Aardema, Verna (1960). *Tales from the story hat*. New York: Coward, McCann.

Aardema, Verna (1975). *Why mosquitoes buzz in people's ears*. Pictures by Leo and Diane Dillon. New York: Dial.

Adoff, Arnold (1970). *Malcolm X*. Illus. by John Wilson. New York: Crowell.

Adoff, Arnold (1973). *Black is brown is tan*. Pictures by Emily McCully. New York: Harper & Row.

Adoff, Arnold (1974). *My black me. a beginning book of black poetry*. New York: Dutton.

Adoff, Arnold ed. (1970). *I am the darker brother: an anthology of modern poems by black Americans*. New York: Macmillan.

Aliki (1965). *A weed is a flower*. Englewood Cliffs, NJ: Prentice-Hall.

Arkhurst, Joyce Cooper (1964). *The adventures of spider*. Boston: Little, Brown.

Armstrong, William (1969). *Sounder*. Illustrated by James Barkley. New York: Harper & Row.

Baker, A. (1967). *We build together*. Champaign, IL: National Council of Teachers of English.

Banks, J. A. & Banks, C. A. M. Banks (1989). *Multicultural education*. Boston: Allyn & Bacon.

Bannerman, Helen (1899). *Little Black Sambo*. New York: Stokes.

Barrett, Joyce Durham (1989). *Willie's not the hugging kind*. New York: Harper & Row.

Beim, Lorraine and Jerrold (1945). *Two is a team*. New York: Harcourt, Brace.

Bontemps, Arna (1941). *Golden slippers an anthology of negro poetry for young readers*. New York: Harper & Row.

Bontemps, Arna (1951). *Chariot in the sky*. Philadelphia, PA: John C. Winston Co.

Bontemps, Arna (1954). *The story of George Washington Carver*. New York: Dunlop.

Bontemps, Arna (1959). *Frederick Douglass*. New York: Knopf.

Bontemps, Arna (1963). *American Negro poetry*. New York: Hill & Wang.

Braune, Anna (1937). *Honey Chile*. New York: Doubleday.

Broderick, D. (1973). *Image of the Black in children's fiction*. New York: R. R. Bowker.

Bunyan, J. (1678). *Pilgrim's progress*. Philadelphia: H. Altemus.

Cameron, Ann (1981). *The stories Julian tells*. Illustrations by Ann Sturgnell. New York: Pantheon Books.

Craft, William (1860). *Running a thousand miles for freedom; or. the escape of William and Ellen Craft from slavery*. London: W. Tweedie. Miami: Mnemosyne Publishing Co. 1969.

Credle, Ellis (1935). *Across the cotton patch*. New York: Thomas Nelson.

Douty, Esther M. (1968). *Forten the sailmaker*. New York: Rand McNally.

Dragonwagon, Cresent (1990). *Homplace*. Illus. by Jerry Pinkney. New York: Macmillan.

Edwards, Harry Stillwell (1920). *Eneas Africanus*. Macon, GA: J. W. Burke Co.Evans, Eva Knox (1935). *Araminta*. New York: Minton, Balch & Co.

Epstein, Sam & Beryl (1961). *George Washington Carver, Negro scientist*. New York: Dell.

Equiano, Olaudah (1789). *The interesting narratives of the life of Olaudah Equiano or Gustavus Vassa the African, written by himself*. London: for the author.

Evans, Eva Knox (1935). *Araminta*. New York: Minton, Balch & Co.

Evans, Eva Knox (1938). *Araminta's goat*. New York: G. P. Putnam's Sons.

Evans, Eva Knox (1947). *All about us*. Irvington, New York: Capitol Publishing Co.

Feelings, Muriel (1971). *Moja means one, Swahili counting book*. Pictures by Tom Feelings. New York: Dial.

Feelings, Muriel (1974). *Jambo means hello. Swahili alphabet book*. Pictures by Tom Feelings. New York: Dial.

Feelings, Tom (1972). *Black pilgrimage.* New York: Lothrop, Lee & Shepard Co.

Feelings, Tom (1978). *Something on my mind.* Words by Nikki Grimes. New York: Dial.

Felton, Harold W. (1966). *Jim Beckworth Negro mountain men.* New York: Dodd, Mead.

Felton, Harold W. (1967). *Edward Rose Negro trail blazer.* New York: Dodd, Mead.

Felton, Harold W. (1969). *Nat Love. Negro cowboy.* New York: Dodd, Mead.

Fisher, Leonard Everett (1970). *Picture book of revolutionary war heroes.* Harrisburg, PA: Stackpole Books.

Flournoy, Valerie (1985). *The patchwork quilt.* Illustrated by Jerry Pinkney. New York: Dial.

Gates, Doris (1951). *Little vic.* New York: Viking Press.

Gray, Genevieve (1974). *Send Wendell.* Drawings by Symeon Shimin. New York: McGraw-Hill.

Greene, Bette (1974). *Philip Hall likes me. I reckon maybe.* New York: Dial.

Greenfield, Eloise (1972). *Honey. I love and other love poems.* Pictures by Leo and Diane Dillon. New York: Crowell.

Greenfield, Eloise (1974). *Sister.* Drawings by Moneta Barnett. New York: Crowell.

Greenfield, Eloise (1978). *Talk about a family.* Illus. by James Calvin. New York: Lippincott.

Greenfield, Eloise (1988). *Grandpa's face.* New York: Philomel books.

Hale, Sarah Josepha (1990). *Mary had a little lamb.* New York: Scholastic.

Hamilton, Virginia (1967). *Zeeley.* Illus. by Symeon Shimin. New York: Macmillan.

Hamilton, Virginia (1971). *The planet of Junior Brown.* New York: Macmillan.

Hamilton, Virginia (1972). *W. E. B. DuBois.* Illus. with photographs. New York: Crowell.

Hamilton, Virginia (1973). *Time-ago lost. more tales of Jahdu.* Illus. by Ray Prother. New York:

Hamilton, Virginia (1974). *M. C. Higgins. the great.* New York: Macmillan.

Hamilton, Virginia (1974). *Paul Robeson. the life and times of a free black man.* Illus. with photographs. New York: Harper & Row.

Hamilton, Virginia (1982). *Sweet whispers. Brother Rush.* New York: Philomel.

Hamilton, Virginia (1985). *The people could fly: American black folktales.* Illustrated by Leo York: Knopf.

Hamilton, Virginia (1988). *In the beginning.* New York: Harcourt, Brace Jovanovich.

Hamilton, Virginia (1989). *The bells of Christmas.* New York: Harcourt Brace Jovanovich.

Hamilton, Virginia C. (1968). *The house of Dies Drear.* New York: Macmillan.

Harris, Joel Chandler (1881). *Uncle Remus tales.* New York: D. Appleton.

Hayes, Florence (1948). *Skid.* Boston: Houghton Mifflin.

Hernandez, H. (1989). *Multicultural education: a teacher's guide to content and process.* Columbus: Merrill.

Hill, Elizabeth Starr (1967). *Evan's corner.* New York: Holt, Rinehart & Winston.

Hogan, Inez (1939). *Mule twins.* New York: E. P. Dutton.

Hogan, Inez (1940). *Nicodemus laughs.* New York: E. P. Dutton & Co.

Hogan, Inez (1942). *Nicodemus runs away.* New York: E. P. Dutton & Co.

Hogan, Inez (1945). *Nicodemus and the goose.* New York: E. P. Dutton & Co.

Hunter, Kristin (1968). *The Soul Brothers and Sister Lou.* New York: Scribner.

Jackson, Jesse (1945). *Call me Charley.* New York: Harper & Row.

Johnson, Angela (1989). *Tell me a story. Mama.* Pictures by David Soman. New York: Orchard Books.

Jordan, June (1970). *The voice of the children.* New York: Holt, Rinehart, and Winston .

Jordan, June (1972). *Fannie Lou Hamer.* Illus. by Albert Williams. New York: Cromell.

Katz, Williams Loren (1977). *Black people who made the old west.* Illus. with photographs. New York: Crowell.

Keats, Ezra Jack (1962). *The snowy day.* New York: Viking.

Keats, Ezra Jack (1967). *Peter's chair.* New York: Harper & Row.

Keats, Ezra Jack (1968). *A letter to Amy.* New York: Harper & Row.

Keats, Ezra Jack (1969). *Goggles.* New York: Macmillan.

Keats, Ezra Jack (1971). *Apt. 3.* New York: Macmillan.

Lanker, Brian (1989). *I dream a world. portraits of black workmen who changed America.* New York: Stewart, Tabori & Co.

Lester, Julius (1968). *To be a slave.* Illustrated by Tom Feelings. New York: Dial.

Lester, Julius (1972). *Long journey home stories from Black history.* New York: Dial.

Lester, Julius (1982). *This strange new feeling.* New York: Dial.

Lester, Julius (1987). *The tales of Uncle Remus: the adventures of Brer Rabbit.* New York: Dial Books.

Lester, Julius (1988). *More tales of Uncle Remus: Further adventures of Brer Rabbit. his friends. Enemies & Others.* New York: Dial Books.

Lindsay, Maud (1922). *Little Missy.* Boston, MA: Lothrop, Lee & Shepard.

Lofting, Hugh (1922). *The voyages of Dr. Dolitle.* New York: A. Stokes Co.

MacCann, D. & Woodard, G. (1985). *The Black American in books for children: readings in racism,* Macmillian

Mathis, Sharon Bell (1974). *Listen for the fig tree.* New York: Viking.

Mathis, Sharon Bell (1975). *The hundred penny boy.* Illus. by Leo and Diane Dillon. New York: Viking.

McGovern, Ann (1969). *Black is beautiful.* New York: Four Winds.

McKissack, Patricia C. (1986). *Flossie and the fox.* New York: Dial.

McKissack, Patricia C. (1988). *Mirandy and Brother Wind.* Illustrated by Jerry Pinkney. New York: The Trumpet Club.

Meadowcraft, Enid L. (1948). *By secret railway.* New York: Crowell.

Means, Florence Crannel (1938). *Shuttered windows.* Illustrated by Armstrong Sperry. Boston: Hougthon Mifflin.

Means, Florence Crannel (1952). *Carver's George. a biography of George Washington Carver.* Boston: Houghton Mifflin.

Meriwether, Louise (1973). *Don't ride the bus on Monday. the Rosa Parks story.* Illus. by David Scott Brown. Englewood Cliffs, NJ: Prentice Hall.

Metucha, N. J.: Scarecrow.

Miles, Miska (1965). *Mississippi possum.* Illustrated by John Schoenherr. Boston: Little, Brown & Co.

Musgrove, Margaret (1976). *Ashanti to Zulu. Africa traditions.* Pictures by Leo and Diane Dillon. New York: Dial.

Myers, Walter Dean (1975). *It ain't all for nothin'.* New York: Viking.

Myers, Walter Dean (1982). *Won't know till I get there.* New York: Viking.

Myers, Walter Dean (1988). *Fallen angels.* New York: Scholastic, Inc.

Myers, Walter Dean (1988). *Me. Mop. and the Moondance Kids.* New York: Delacorte Press.

Myers, Walter Dean (1988). *Scorpions.* New York: Harper.

Myers, Walter Dean (1990). *The mouse rap.* New York: Harper.

Northrup, Solomon (1853). *Twelve years a slave.* Auburn: Derby and Miller. (microfiche. Chicago: Library Resources, 1970). LAC 14193.

Ortiz, Victoria (1974). *Sojourner Truth. a self-made woman.* Philadelphia: J. B. Lippincourt.

Page, Thomas Nelson (1887). *In ole Virginia.* New York: A. Scribner's Sons.

Page, Thomas Nelson (1888). *Two little confederates.* New York: Charles A. Scribner's Sons.

Petersham, Maud and Miska (1936). *The story book of sugar.* Philadelphia, PA: John C. Winston.

Petersham, Maud and Miska (1939). *The story book of cotton.* Philadelphia, PA: John C. Winston.

Pyrnelle, Louise-Clarke (1917) . *Miss Li'l' Tweety.* Nashville: Fisk University, African-American Heritage Library Collection.

Pyrnelle, Louise-Clarke. (1883). *Diddle. Dumps & Tot or plantation child-life.* New York: Charles A.

Radford, Ruby L. (1973). *Mary McLeod Bethune.* Illus. by Lydia Rosiie. New York: Putnams Sons.

Ramsey, P. & Williams, L. R. (1989). *Multicultural education: a sourcebook.* New York: Garland.

Rollock, B. (1988). *Black authors and illustrators of children's books.* New York: Garland.

San Souci, Robert D . (1989) . *The talking tree* . Illus . by Jerry Pinkney. New York: Dial.

Scott, Ann Herbert (1967). *Sam.* Illustrated by Symeon Shimin. New York: McGraw-Hill.

Scribner's Sons.

Sharpe, Stella Gentry (1939). *Tobe.* Chapel Hill, NC: University of North Carolina Press.

Steptoe, John (1969). *Stevie.* New York: Harper & Row.

Steptoe, John (1980). *Daddy is a monster...sometimes.* New York: Lippincott.

Steptoe, John (1987). *Mufaro's beautiful daughters: an African tale.* New York: Lothrop.

Sterling, Dorothy (1958). *Captain of the planter. the story of Robert Smalls.* New York: Doubleday & Co.

Sterling, Dorothy (1959). *Mary Jane.* New York: Doubleday.

Sterling, Dorothy (1964). *Lucretia Mott. gentle warrior.* New York: Doubleday.

Stoltz, Mary (1988). *Storm in the night.* New York: Harper & Row.

Tarry, Ellen (1946). *My dog Rinty.* New York: Viking.

Tarry, Ellen (1967). *Young Jim: The early years of James Weldon*

Johnson. New York: Dodd, Mead.

Thomas, Ianthe (1973). *Lordy. Aunt Hattie.* Pictures by Thomas di Grazia. New York: Harper & Row.

Twain, Mark (1884). *Adventures of Huckleberry Finn.* New York: Harper.

Upton, Bertha (1895). *The adventures of two dutch girls and a golliwog.* Illustrated by Florence Upton. London: Longmans.

Warwick, Mary (1989). *Alabama angels.* Montgomery, AL: Blackbelt Press.

Weaver, Annie Vaughan (1930). *Frawg.* Philadelphia, PA: J. B. Lippincott.

Wilkinson, Brenda (1975). *Ludell.* New York: Harper & Row.

Yates, Elizabeth (1950). *Amos Fortune. free man.* New York: Alladin Books.

Since the Sixties: Literature for Children by African-American Writers and Illustrators

Frances Smith Foster, Ph.D.
University of California, San Diego

Through all history, ancient and modern; each land, each nation, impresses most painstakingly upon the rising generation the fact that it possesses a history and a literature, and that it must live up to the traditions of its history, and make that literature a part of its life...

Assuredly we will teach our boys and girls, not only their own history and literature, but works by their own authors.

Alice Dunbar-Nelson 1922

This essay intends to sketch the development of literature for children and young adults by African-Americans since the 1960s. It begins, however, with a quote from the 1920s because this helps support my thesis that the significance of literature as a wellspring of pride and purpose for African-American children was not an idea invented out of the passion of the Civil Rights and Black Power eras. The outcries for literary and curricular reform that form a crucial part of those movements heralded a renaissance of writing directed towards black children but they were merely renewals of calls that had been issued since the beginnings of the written African-American literary tradition. Numerous writers and educators have argued that literacy must be developed and exercised by literature that reflects the realities of African-American culture, literature that not only taught young readers about themselves and their places in the world but encouraged their imaginations and their own creative aspirations.

During the antebellum and the Reconstruction periods, African-Americans understood the importance of literature for children and young adults written for, by, and about African-Americans. During the mid-nineteenth and early twentieth centuries, literature for African-American children was a special concern for numerous constituencies. Abolitionist newspapers, for example, often included children's columns that featured poems, stories, and essays. The black religious press developed works suitable for use in Sunday Schools and classrooms designed to teach values and morals and using characters, settings, and situations with which black children and youth could readily identify. A few periodicals were created exclusively for young African-American readers. Most prominent of these were *Joy* (1887), *Ivy* (1888), and *The Brownie's Book* (1920). And, to an extent far greater than today, African-American writers generally expected children and young adults to be a significant part of their readership. Works such as Josephine Brown's *Biography of an American Bondman* (1856), Amelia E. Johnson's *Clarence and Corinne* (1890), and Frances Ellen Watkins Harper's *Iola Leroy* (1892) were designed to instruct, to motivate, and to please readers of all ages. In *Iola Leroy*, for example, Harper says she wove "of fact and fiction" a work which she hoped would "awaken in the hearts of our countrymen a strong sense of justice and a more Christlike humanity..." and which, she explicitly states, she hopes would "inspire the children."[1] Historian and social activist, William Still, emphasized this point in the preface to that novel by noting that "the thousands of colored Sunday-schools...casting about for an interesting, moral story-book, full of practical lessons, will not be content to be without 'Iola Leroy'" (Harper, 3).

When Alice Dunbar-Nelson reaffirmed the importance of literature for and about African-American children, she also stated the importance of at least some of these literary works being by African-American writers. Such writings not only teach young people their social and aesthetic history, but they help motivate them to aspire to similar achievements. They help instill a sense of racial pride in the artistic achievements of their own culture. Such writings verify for black children that they, too, can wield the pen for pleasure and for profit. And, while Dunbar-Nelson doesn't say this directly, familiarity with works from their own culture give African-American children touchstones against which they can evaluate, interpret and compare writings by those from other racial and ethnic backgrounds. And, Dunbar-Nelson's statement also emphasizes a correlating point, since literature for African-American children is so important, we must not consider it to be a lesser literature, we must not lower our standards and accept inferior writing. It is no more helpful to celebrate or to tolerate mediocre or pernicious writings by African-Americans than it is to accept it from writers of any other group.

The publication of literature for children by African-Americans, while included in the first spring of literary outpourings and never totally ceasing, has not been a continuous stream but one of spurts and dribbles. It is not that artistic interest or abilities come in floods or droughts but that the flow of publications is also controlled by economic, political and social factors. Since African-Americans have rarely controlled the publishing and distribution outlets, the availability of literature for African-American children has generally been dependent upon the national interest in and toleration for African-American generally. Thus, during the forties and fifties when the children's literature was becoming a discrete genre and, perhaps even more significantly, a separate "market," virtually no African-Americans writers or characters were to be found in the "juvenile divisions" that were popping up in every major publishing house. The handful of African-American writers who managed to get their works for young adults and for children into print were mainly those such as Countee Cullen, Langston Hughes, Arna Bontemps, Gwendolyn Brooks, and Ellen Tarry who had first established their literary reputation in other fields.

In 1954, *Brown vs. The Board of Education* desegregated the public schools but a full ten years later, blacks were still not accepted in "The All-White World of Children's Books." In her landmark essay by that title, Nancy Larrick revealed that only 4/5 of 1% of the 5, 206 children's trade books published between 1962 and 1964 included an African-American character. Of these 44, 12 were picture books that included African-Americans in the illustrations but did not mention them in the text.[2]

Since the sixties, however, that has changed. In 1979, a similar survey indicated that 14.4% of all children's books published between

1973 and 1975 included at least one black character. While this figure includes references to or pictures of black people from every
nationality and it is not limited to books by African-Americans, it is
a substantial increase over the 4/5 of 1% in the mid sixties. Though
the African-American writers and illustrators who have been published since the sixties form a distinct minority of this literary out-
put, nonetheless, publishing opportunities for African-Americans
have increased, and, more importantly, while their actual numbers
are relatively small, their effect upon children's literature has been
large indeed. Since the sixties, the steady trickle of literature by more
or less established African-American writers for young people, writers such as Ann Petry, Jesse Jackson, and Lorenz Graham, was aug-
mented by a new generation of talented writers and illustrators who
for the next decade contributed a stream of children's literature
infused with a distinctly black perspective.

Some, such as James Baldwin, June Jordan, Nikki Giovanni,
Toni Cade Bambara, Alice Childress, Lucille Clifton, Rosa Guy,
Alice Walker, and Julius Lester are also acclaimed writers for adult
audiences. Others such as Walter Dean Myers, Sharon Belle Mathis,
Eloise Greenfield, Virginia Hamilton, James Haskins, Joyce, Hansen,
Patricia McKissack, Lillie Patterson, John Shearer Mildred Taylor,
John Steptoe, Mildred Pitts Walter, Brenda Wilkinson, and Camille
Yarborough publish primarily for young readers.

While their subjects, themes, styles and intended audiences varied considerably, until recently most writers who wrote primarily for
children and young adults have worked within the genre called "realistic fiction" and they have focussed upon contemporary urban
ghetto experiences east of the Mississippi and north of the Ohio. The
preponderance of urban ghetto stories that characterized the late
sixties and the seventies privileged one aspect of the African-
American experience and came close to replacing stereotypes with
new stereotypes; however, these books generally celebrated the
strength, resourcefulness and love of those black communities, exemplified the richness and poetry of their language, and introduced
complexities of characterization that avoided the surface or negative
stereotypes which permeated much of the work produced by out-
siders. For example, James Baldwin's *Little Man, Little Man* (1976)
is about JT, an imaginative six year old, and his two friends WT and
Blinky. The youngsters live in a Harlem neighborhood peopled with
a variety of colorful characters. While some of the children's neighbors are alcoholics and junkies, others are hard working fathers who

take their kids to the beach on their days off and who make cocoa for their children's friends. And when WT is seriously cut by a broken bottle, it is the alcoholic wife of the moody janitor who tenderly bandages his wound and soothes the children's fears.

Other works such as Lorenz Graham's *North Town* are about blacks who were beginning to integrate themselves into the American Dream Society. In Graham's book, for example, young David and his family move to North Town and after some initial difficulties they find friends and the promise of acceptance into the previously all-white neighborhood. Graham's sequel, *Whose Town?* published in 1969 recognized the complexities of integration and the likelihood that racial tensions would not be so quickly assuaged. In this story, David is beaten by a white gang, he is harassed by police, and he is faced with the question of joining a separatist organization.

Walter Dean Myers got his start by winning the Council on Interracial Books for Children's first context for unpublished Third World writers in 1969 with a picture book *Where Does the Day Go?* His next two books were fantasies for younger children but with *Fast Sam, Cool Clyde, and Stuff* (1975) which was an American Library Award selection, Myers established himself as the Dean of realistic fiction for young adults. Walter Dean Myers' books have repeatedly been selected as ALA Notables and ALA Best Books for Young Adults. *Scorpions*, Myers' 1988 portrayal of a young man's brush with gang warfare was named a Newbery Honor Book and *Fallen Angels*, his candid portrayal of teen-age soldiers in Vietnam gained him his third Coretta Scott King Award. Myers writes most often of the Harlem, New York neighborhood in which he was raised, a neighborhood that he describes as "a place of affirmation. [Where] The excitement of city living exploded in the teeming streets." Myers' goals are representative of those that most African-American writers for children have expressed. He summarizes his feelings this way: "As a black writer I want to talk about my people. I want to tell the reader about an old Black man I knew who told me he was God. I want to tell the reader how a blind man feels when he was God. I want to tell the reader how a blind man feels when he hears that he is not wanted because he is Black. I want to tell Black children about their humanity and about their history and how to grease their legs so the ash won't show and how to braid their hair so it's easy to comb on frosty winters mornings."[3] Walter Dean Myers writes of teen age love in *Motown and Didi* (1984), of the treachery of sports in *Hoops* (1981) and the perils of stardom in

Crystal (1987), of adoption and aging in *Won't Know Till I Get There* (1981), and of little league baseball in *Me, Mop, and the Moondance Kid* (1988). Though Harlem is his favorite setting, some of his stories take place on midwestern college campuses and in the jungles of Peru. While his mastery of the urban realism is unchallenged, he sometimes writes fantasy, folktales, and nonfiction.

While realism dominated the fiction of the seventies and continues to be a significant genre today, another significant occurrence since the sixties was the increase in works that evoked the African and the African-American heritages as positive and ennobling experiences. In 1964, Julius Lester published *To Be A Slave* (1964), a collection of stories about slavery as told by slaves themselves and illustrated by Tom Feelings. The book was named a runner-up for the Newbery Prize. Two other works of this type by Lester are *Long Journey Home: Stories from Black History* (1972) and *This Strange New Feeling* (1982). Virginia Hamilton's *Zeely* (1967) is a sensitive story that centers around a beautiful and mysterious woman who Zeely believes must be an African queen. She followed that work with *The House of Dies Drear* (1968), a story of the underground railroad. Virginia Hamilton has continuously returned to themes of African and African-American culture with works such as *The Time Ago Tales of Jahdu* (1969), *Time-Ago Lost: More Tales of Jahdu* (1973), *The Magical Adventures of Pretty Pearl* (1983), *The Mystery of Dies Drear* (1987), and *The People Could Fly: American Black Folktales* (1985). African and African-American culture has continued to be important themes in the nineties. Three especially noteworthy examples are Leontyne Price's retelling of the opera, *Aida* (1990), Tom Feeling's *Tommy Traveler in the World of Black History* (1991), and Ashley Bryan's *All Night, All Day: A Child's First Book of African-American Spirituals* (1991). Gloriously illustrated by Leo and Diane Dillon, the text of *Aido*, makes clear the Ethiopian heritage of the princess that Price's own performances have made unforgettable. Feelings on the other hand, has looked not to the "elite" culture of the classic operas but to "mass" culture of comic books for inspiration. *Tommy Traveler* is an anthology of the lives and times of famous African-Americans done in the format of a comic book but with illustrations and text far superior to most. Feelings has made a bold, and in retrospect entirely logical, move towards offering interesting and serious literature in a form that appeals to both avid and reluctant readers. And, Bryan frames the text and music for several important songs of our past with excellent art and commentary.

One of the best writers of historical fiction is Mildred D. Taylor, whose stories about Cassie Logan who according to a *New York Times* reviewer "bids fair to become a folk favorite on the level of Huckleberry Finn" and "creates its own place next to such classics as Wilder's *Little House on the Prairie.*" The first of the series, *Roll of Thunder, Hear My Cry* won the Newbery Medal, was nominated for the National Book Award, and was runner up for several other prestigious prizes. Taylor won a Coretta Scott King Award and earned a second National Book Award nomination with the second Logan family story, *Let the Circle Be Unbroken. Let the Circle Be Unbroken* was also an ALA Notable Book, an ALA Best Book for Young Adults, and one of *The New York Times* Outstanding Books of the Year. *Song of the Trees* was another *The New York Times* Outstanding Book and the *Boston Globe-Horn Book* award went to the fourth Cassie Logan book, *The Friendship. The Gold Cadillac* (1987) won the Christopher Award and in 1988, the Children's Book Council gave Mildred D. Taylor a special commendation "for a body of work that has examined significant social issues and presented them in outstanding books for young readers." Taylor's fifth in the Logan family saga, *The Road to Memphis*, was published in 1990, the same year that she also gave us another thoughtful work, *Mississippi Bridge.* Other important works that use African and African-American history themes include Lucille Clifton's *All Us Come Across the Water* (1973), Sharon Bell Mathis' *Listen for the Fig Tree* (1974) and Margaret W. Musgrove's *Ashanti to Zulu: African Traditions* (1976), Patricia C. McKissack's *Mirandy and Brother Wind* (1988), and William Hooks's *The Ballad of Belle Dorcas* (1990).

Since the sixties, there has been a noticeable increase in non-fiction by African-Americans. Works such as *Mojo Means One: A Swahili Counting Book* (1971) and *Jambo Means Hello: A Swahili Alphabet* (1974) were quite popular and remain in print today. Since the late eighties, the Afro-Bets series has become a favorite for very young readers. A few plays such as *Escape to Freedom: A Play About Young Frederick Douglass* (1978) and *Langston, A Play* (1982) have appeared in print. Poetry has been a less popular genre but since the sixties several collections of poetry have established themselves as children's classics. *Boys and Girls of Bronzeville* by Pulitzer Prize winner Gwendolyn Brooks is one of the few early efforts to be reprinted. Ms. Brooks also contributed a new title *The Tiger Who Wore White Gloves: Or, What You Are You Are* (1974). Eloise Greenfield's *Honey I Love* may be the most enduring of the seventies creations. Other poets whose works have proved to be quite popular with younger readers are Leslie Little, Nikki Giovanni, Mari Evans, and June Jordan.

The most popular genre of nonfiction is the biography. Most African-American biographies concentrate upon celebrities in sports and entertainment. But a significant number are about important African-Americans from other walks of life. In addition to a multitude of books about Dr. Martin Luther King, Jr., Sojourner Truth, and Harriet Tubman, there are many that recreate the lives and times of less well known or more historical figures. These include Ann Petry's *Tituba of Salem Village* (1964), Louise Meriwether's *The Freedom Ship of Robert Small* (1971), *The Heart Man: Dr. Daniel Hale Williams* (1972) and *Don't Ride the Bus on Monday: The Rosa Parks Story* (1973); Virginia Hamilton's *W.E.B. Du Bois: A Biography* (1972) and *Paul Robeson: The Life and Times of a Free Black Man* (1974); and Lillie Patterson's *Benjamin Banneker: Genius of Early America* (1978) and *Coretta Scott King* (1977). The trend has continued in the eighties and nineties. Among the more exciting recent biographies are Virginia Hamilton's *Anthony Burns: The Defeat and Triumph of a Fugitive Slave* (1988) and Patricia and Frederick McKissack's *Long Hard Journey: The Story of the Pullman Porter* (1990).

The most prolific African-American writers of non-fiction for children and youth is James Haskins, a Phi Beta Kappa graduate of Georgetown and Professor of English at the University of Florida. Professor Haskins also writes for adults, but he concentrates upon the younger readers because as he so rightly says, "adults either read or do not read depending on how they felt about books when they were young." Haskin's biographies are intended to be accurate but also interesting and exciting enough to encourage young people to become life-long readers. An idea of the range of people that Haskins writes about can be found from the following titles: *The Picture Life of Malcolm X* (1975), *The Story of Stevie Wonder* (1976), *Bob McAdoo, Superstar* (1978), *Barbara Jordan* (1979), *Andrew Young: A Man with a Mission* (1979), *From Lew Alcindor to Kareem Abdul-Jabbar*, *"Magic": A Biography of Earvin Johnson* (1982), *Lena Horne* (1983), *Donna Summer* (1983), *Bill Cosby: America's Most Famous Father* (1988), and *Mr. Bojangles: The Biography of Bill Robinson* (1988). Jim Haskins has also produced remarkable group biographies such as *Black Music in America: A History Through Its People* (1987) and *Black Dance in America: A History Through Its People* (1990).

It was well after the sixties that the juries of the most prestigious prizes in children's literature began to acknowledge the talents of

African-American writers. The most lauded writer is Virginia Hamilton, whose publication of *M.C. Higgins, The Great* (1974) made her the first individual to win both the Newbery Medal and the National Book Award with the same work. *M.C. Higgins, The Great*, a sensitive and challenging story of the coming of age of a young black boy in rural Ohio, also won the *Boston Globe-Horn Book Award* and the Lewis Carroll Shelf Award. Since then Virginia Hamilton has won the Coretta Scott King Award twice, the *Boston Globe-Horn Book* again, the Edgar Allan Poe Award, the Ohioana Book Award, and two Newbery Honor Book awards. She has become such a major figure in children's literature that there is a national conference held annually at Bowling Green State University in her name and she has been named Distinguished Visiting Professor at both Queens College and the Ohio State University.

It is a special gift when one can become renown as both writer and illustrator and John Steptoe was one of the few African-Americans to achieve this. His career began at age sixteen with the self-illustrated book *Stevie* (1969). Among the works that he has written and illustrated are *My Special Best Words* (1974), *The Daddy is a Monster...Sometimes* (1980), *The Story of Jumping Mouse* (1984), and *Mufaro's Beautiful Daughters* (1987), the latter book was featured in an episode of the Bill Cosby Show. Before his early death, John Steptoe had worked with award winning writers such as Lucille Clifton, Eloise Greenfield, and Rosa Guy. Among his many prizes are the Society of Illustrators Gold Medal (1970), The Coretta Scott King Award (1981), and the Caldecott Honor Book Award (1985).

Along with his partner Diane Dillon, Leo Dillon won the Caldecott Medal for two consecutive years, first in 1976 for *Why Mosquitoes Buzz in People's Ears* and again in 1977 for *Ashanti to Zulu*. The Dillons' illustrations in Sharon Bell Mathis' *The Hundred Penny Box* (1975), Eloise Greenfield's *Honey, I Love* (1978), Mildred Pitts Walter's *Brother to the Wind*, and Virginia Hamilton's *The People Could Fly* (1985) are among their best.

Jerry Pinckney is another individual who has been successful in many areas, but for whom children's literature is a major priority. Pinckney is an art professor at the University of Delaware whose work has been displayed world-wide. He has illustrated record albums, magazine covers, and U.S. postage stamps (including the Martin Luther king, Jr. and the Harriet Tubman stamps). Jerry Pinckney is a 1989 Caldecott Honor Book Artist and the only illustrator to have won the Coretta Scott King Award three times. *The*

Patchwork Quilt which he illustrated for Valerie Flournoy was not only a Coretta Scott King winner but also an IRA-CBC Children's Choice, An ALA Notable Book, a Reading Rainbow Selection, and a Christopher Ward winner. Pinckney's recent contributions include *Mirandy and Brother Wind* (1988), *The Green Loin of Zion Street* (1988) *Homeplace* (1990) and *Pretend You're a Cat* (1990).

Illustrator Tom Feelings has worked for the government of Guyana as a consultant on children's literature and has taught art in that country. Among his many honors are the Coretta Scott King Award for his illustrations in Nikki Grimes' *Something on My Mind* (1979) and an honorable mention in the same competition for his work with Eloise Greenfield called *Daydreamers* (1982). Other notable illustrators include Pat Cummings, Donald Crews, and the incredible Jacob Lawrence whose *Harriet and the Promised Land* (1968) has become a collector's item.

Contemporary African-American children's literature spans every genre and every age category. Books such as *Stevie*, *Mojo Means One*, *I Can Do It Myself*, *Cornrows*, and *The Patchwork Quilt* are particularly interesting to preschoolers. Others such as *Circle of Gold*, *The Gift Giver*, *Paris*, *Pee Wee and Me*, *About Michael Jackson*, and *The Golden Serpent* might appeal more to primary school children. Junior and Senior High students particularly enjoy works with teen age protagonists. Among the many fine works are *Marked by Fire*, *Roll of Thunder Hear My Cry*, *A Teacup of Roses*, *Generations*, *The Lucky Stone*, *Rainbow Jordan*, *Forever Friends*, and *A Hero Ain't Nothin But a Sandwich*. But these and most books defy age categories and are joyfully read by adults and children of all ages.

Despite the several titles from the last fifteen years referenced above, since the eighties, the stream of books for children by African-Americans has slowed to a mere trickle. Many books are out of print and new titles are few and far between. Only about 1% of children's books published in the first half of 1980s focus upon African-Americans and many of those are not by African-Americans. New vocations, retirement, or death have taken the talents of Lorenz Graham, John Steptoe, and others. Established writers such as Hamilton, Myers, Clifton, Guy, and Greenfield continue to publish regularly but new writers are relatively few and fewer still have published works that break new ground since the sixties. Exceptions include Joyce Carol Thomas, whose stories set in her native Oklahoma have attracted very positive attention and Mildred Pitts Walter who subtly reverses sexist stereotypes in *Justin and the Best*

Baked Biscuits in the World, a chronicle of the summer of a young boy with his grandfather when among the lessons learned are the joys of cooking. Other new, talented writers and illustrators who are replenishing the supply and despite tremendous odds are making serious contributions to the genre are Dolores Johnson, Joyce Hansen, Emily Moore, Eleanora Tate, Candy Boyd, and Angela Johnson. Dori Sanders' first book, *Clover* (1990), an unusual coming of age story about a young Georgia girl and her adjustment to life with her white stepmother, was a *New York Times* best seller. And from the ranks of established writers and artists for adults are coming the contributions of Faith Ringgold (*Tar Beach*, 1991), Alice Walker (*Finding the Green Stone*, 1991), and Sherely Anne Williams (*Picking Cotton*, forthcoming).

At a moment when the percentage of people of color in the United States is becoming a majority, when the public schools in many districts are predominantly African-American, and when children's and young adult literature is enjoying its greatest popularity, the amount of literature for children and young adults by and about African-Americans continues to decline. How long or how serious that current trend will be depends in part upon us. If we read, buy, and demand quality literature by African-Americans for our children, it will be made available. The talent is now, as it has always been, waiting for the opportunity to make itself known. And, to paraphrase Alice Ruth Dunbar-Nelson and countless others who have testified, we must continually teach our children and ourselves, not only our own history and literature, but that history and literature as presented by our own authors. In so doing we will ensure the continued awareness of and pride in our own literary productions, a sense of literary values, and perhaps most importantly increased hopes in the literary possibilities of our future. It is, after all, our writers who, as Virginia Hamilton says: "deal in possibilities, not with what is but what might become."

Notes

1. New York: Oxford University Press, 1988, p. 282. Subsequent references are from this edition and found in the text.
2. *Saturday Review* (1965), p. 64.
3. *Something About the Author Autobiographical Series.* Vol 2. p. 155.

Works Cited

Aardema, Verna. *Why Mosquitoes Buzz in People's Ears*. Illus. Leo and Diane Dillon. New York:Dial, 1976.

Brooks, Gwendolyn. *Bronzeville Boys and Girls* New York: Harper, 1956.

___. *The Tiger Who Wore White Gloves*. Chicago: Third World Press, 1974.

Brown, Josephine. *Biography of an American Bondman* (1856). Reprinted in *Two Biographies by African-American Women*. New York: Oxford UP, 1991.

Baldwin, James. *Little Man. Little Man: A Story of Childhood*. Ills. Yoran Cazac. New York: Dial, 1976.

Bryan, Ashley. *All Night. All Day: A Child's First Book of African-American Spirituals*. New York: Writers and Readers, 1 9 9 1 .

Clifton, Lucille. *All Us Come Across the Water*. Illus. John Steptoe. New York: Holt, 1973.

Davis, Ossie. *Escape to Freedom: A Play About Frederick Douglass*. New York: Viking, 1978.

___. *Langston. a Play*. New York: Delacorte, 1982.

Feelings, Muriel. *Mojo Means One: Swahili Counting Book*. Illus. Tom Feelings. New York: Dial, 1971.

Feelings, Tom. *Tommy Traveler in the World of Black History*. New York: Writers and Readers, 1991.

Flournoy, Valeria. *The Patchwork Quilt*. Illus. Leo and Diane Dillon. New York: Dial, 1985.

Graham, Lorenz. *North Town*. New York: Crowell, 1965.

___. *Whose Town?* New York: Crowell, 1969.

Greenfield, Eloise. *Honey I Love and Other Poems*. New York: Crowell, 1974.

Hamilton, Virginia. *Anthony Burns. The Defeat and Triumph of a Fugitive Slave*. New York: Knopf, 1988.

___. *The House of Dies Drear*. New York: Macmillan, 1968.

___. *The Magical Adventures of Pretty Pearl*. New York: Harper and Row, 1983.

___. *M.C. Higgins. the Great*. New York: Macmillan, 1974.

___. *The Mystery of Dies Drear*. New York: Greenwillow, 1987.

___. *Paul Robeson: The Life and Times of a Free Black Man*. New York: Harper and Row, 1974.

___. *The People Could Fly*. Illus. Leo and Diane Dillon. New York: Knopf, 1985.

___. *The Long Ago Tales of Jahdu*. Illus. Ray Prather. New York: Macmillan, 1973.

___. *W.E.B. DuBois: A Biography*. New York: Crowell, 1972.

____. *Zeely.* New York: Macmillan, 1967.

Harper, Frances Ellen Watkins. *Iola Leroy.* (1892). New York: Oxford University Press, 1988.

Haskins, James. *Andrew Young: Man With a Mission.* New York: Lothrop, 1979. .

____ *Barbara Jordan.* New York: Dial, 1977.

____. *Bill Cosby: America's Most Famous Father.* New York: Walker, 1988.

____. *Black Music in America: A History Through Its People.* New York: Crowell, 1987.

____. *Black Dance in America: A History Through Its People.* New York: Crowell, 1990.

____. *Bob McAdoo. Superstar.* New York: Morrow, 1987.

____. *From Lew Alcinder to Kareem Abdul Jabbar.* New York: Lothrop, Lee and Shepard, 1978. .

____ *Magic: A Biography of Earvin Johnson.* New York: Enslow, 1982.

____. *The Picture Life of Malcolm X.* New York: Franklin Watts, 1975.

Haskins, James with Kathleen Benson. *Lena: A Personal and Professional Biography of Lena Horne.* New York: Stein and Day, 1984.

____. *The Stevie Wonder Scrapbook.* New York: Grosset and Dunlop, 1978.

Haskins, Jim and N.R. Mitang- *Mr. Bojangles: The Biography of Bill Robinson.* New York: William Morrow, 1988.

Haskins, Jim and J.M. Stifle. *Donna Summer: An Unauthorized Biography.* Boston: Little, Brown, 1988.

Hooks, William. *The Ballad of Belle Dorcas.* Illus. Brian Pinckney. New York: Knopf, 1990.

Johnson, Amelia E. *Clarence and Corrine.* (1890). New York: Oxford UP, 1988.

Larrick, Nancy. The All White World of Children's Books. *Saturday Review of Books.* September 11, 1965.

Lester, Julius. *Long Journey Home.* New York: Dial, 1962.

____. *This Strange New Feeling.* New York: Dial, 1982.

____. *To Be a Slave.* Illus. Tom Feelings. New York: Dial, 1968.

Mathis, Sharon Bell. *The Hundred Penny Box.* Illus. Leo and Diane Dillon. New York: Viking, 1975.

____. *Listen for the Fig Tree.* New York: Viking, 1974.

McKissack, Patricia. *Mirandy and Brother Wind.* Illus. Jerry Pinckney. New York: Knopf, 1988.

McKissack, Patricia and Frederick McKissack. *A Long Hard Journey: The Story of the Pullman Porter.* New York: Walker, 1989.

Meriwether, Louise. *Don't Ride the Bus on Monday.* New York:

Prentice-Hall, 1973.

____. *The Freedom Ship of Robert Small*. New York: Prentice-Hall, 1971.

____. *The Heart Man: Dr. Daniel Hale Williams*. New York: Prentice-Hall, 1972.

Musgrove, Margaret W. *Ashanti to Zulu: African Traditions*. Illus. Leo and Diane Dillon. New York: Dial, 1976.

Myers, Walter Dean. *Crystal*. New York: Viking, 1987.

____. *Fallen Angels*. New York: Scholastic, 1988.

____. *Fast Sam. Cool Clyde and Stuff*. New York: Viking, 1975.

____. *Me, Mop and the Moondance Kid*. New York: Delacorte, 1988.

____. *Motown and Didi: A Love Story*. New York: Viking, 1984.

____. *Scorpions*. New York: Harper and Row, 1988.

____. *Won't Know Til I Get There*. New York: Viking, 1982.

Patterson, Lillie. *Benjamin Banneker: Genius of Early America*. New York: Abingdon, 1978.

____. *Coretta Scott King*. Champaign, Il.: Garrard, 1977.

Petry, Ann. *Tituba of Salem Village*. New York: Crowell, 1964.

Price, Leotyne. *Aida*. Illus. Diane and Leo Dillon. New York: Gulliver, 1990.

Ringgold, Faith. *Tar Beach*. New York: Crown, 1991.

Sanders, Dori. *Clover*. Chapel Hill, N.C.: Algonquin Books, 1990.

Steptoe, John. *Daddy is a Monster. . . Sometimes*. New York: Lippincott, 1980.

____. *Mufaro's Beautiful Daughters*. New York: Lothrop, Lee and Shepard, 1987.

____. *Stevie*. New York: Harper and Row, 1969.

____. *The Story of Jumping Mouse*. New York: Lothrop, Lee and Shepard, 1984.

Taylor, Mildred D. *The Friendship*. New York: Dial, 1987.

____. *The Gold Cadillac*. New York: Dial, 1987.

____. *Let the Circle Be Unbroken*. New York: Dial, 1981.

____. *Mississippi Bridge*. New York: Dial, 1990 .

____. *The Road to Memphis*. New York: Dial, 1990.

____. *Roll of Thunder, Hear My Cry*. New York: Bantam, 1978.

____. *Song of the Trees*. Illus. Jerry Pinckney. New York: Dial, 1975.

Walker, Alice. *Finding the Greenstone*. San Diego: Harcourt, Brace, Jovanovich, 1991.

Walter, Mildred Pitts. *Brother to the Wind*. Illus. Leo and Diane Dillon. New York: Lothrop, 1985.

Williams, Sherely Anne. *Working Cotton*. San Diego: Harcourt, Brace Jovanovich, forthcoming.

Illustration Is My Form, The Black Experience, My Story and My Content

Tom Feelings
University of South Carolina

When I am asked what kind of work I do, my answer is that I am an illustrator, a storyteller, in picture form, who tries to reflect and interpret life as I see it. When I'm asked who I am, I say I am an African who was born in America. Both answers connect me specifically with my past and present. For I believe I bring to my work a quality which is rooted in the culture of Africa and expanded by the experience of being Black in America.

Storytelling is an ancient African tradition where the values and history of a people are passed on to the young verbally. To me, illustrated books are a natural extension of this African oral tradition. Books are wonderful tools, and art, for children which can affect, and have the ability to intensify children's perceptions of reality and stimulate their imagination in a creative way. They can also teach racism and reinforce self-hatred and stereotypes. The best illustrated books can stretch a child's mind and strengthen a child's spirit, preparing the child to face reality and reject the shallow and slick.

Good art that projects the truth can produce a lasting effect on the beholder. A good Black book, can bring some balance to a children's book world, that until the late 1960s was practically lily white. Increasingly, since the sixties, black artists and writers have brought to children's literature a quality already steeped in the Black tradition.

The Black tradition has provided entertainment, passed on messages, communicated our fears, hopes dreams and fantasies, our explanation of the world, our vision of reality, and sense of truth. Black writers and artists have awakened in their viewers a sense of awe, wonder, and participation in the beautiful mystery of Black life and our struggle to survive. For Black Americans, struggle has been an unavoidable condition, and pain, a constant companion.

To me, pain and joy are the two strongest opposing forces affecting the lives of Blacks living in America. As an artist, I have long subscribed to the dictum of Jean Toomer, a Black writer, who said that "an artist is he who can balance strong contrast, who can combine opposing forms and forces in significant unity." For me, a significant part of our Black heritage in America and a driving force in my own work is that constant combining and balancing of seemingly unequal forces.

Until the late 1960s we had little access to the form of children's books, so we could not influence their content. Our history here in America, and in large part ever since we arrived from Africa, has been one of denial and oppression. Yet we brought something with us on those slave ships four hundred years ago, and we haven't lost it. It is our rhythmic energy, our emotional power, our dance-consciousness, our way of turning all knowledge into a living experience. These are expressed very clearly in our music the blues, the spirituals, and jazz.

Black music was the one vector of African culture that proved to be impossible to eradicate. It signified the continuity of Black culture and flourished, even through slavery and segregation. Black music was encoded with a multitude of spiritual messages which have been handed down from generation to generation until the present. That's why our music tends to be both spiritual and political; it has an enormous burden to bear. Our whole artistic experience has been informed by the musical experience which is seen as style a style that is evident in everything we have gotten into and that includes the writing and illustrating of children's books.

Some time ago a teacher of a children's literature class in California gave me a copy of a paper one of her students (an Hispanic woman) had written about my work. She wrote:

> As an illustrator of children's literature, Tom Feelings' use of the dark colors: black, gray, and brown are impressive, yet different. His drawings of the people and the landscapes are attractive and open. The art is not conclusive and encourages the mind to add detail if desired, or color if needed... He creates a mood for the audience to complete.

I could have kissed her, for that is *exactly* what I was trying to do...with subtle suggestion. We Blacks sometimes refer to this as "signifying." An important part of the Black oral tradition in this country, signifying is also a vital aspect of the blues. To signify is to believe in the ability of another person to hear or see what you have to say. The speaker/musician draws the listener in and they complete the image, or the thought, thereby participating in the act.

Black music created this language and I have learned from this and applied it to my art. Sometimes I purposely choose restrictive colors to work with. The great jazz trumpeter, Miles Davis, also does this when, having chosen a corny Walt Disney tune, "Someday My Prince Will Come," then proceeds to expand on it within the limited framework, changing it, opening it up, turning it around, showing us, as in our past, the ability of Black people to creatively go beyond even forced limitations. It's called "improvising within a restricted form." For me, in the late sixties, all the color in books, screaming at you everywhere, competing for space, was too much. So I chose to limit my colors. It was my way of speaking, of pulling my audience in quietly.

In *Moja Means One* and *Jambo Means Hello* I tried to incorporate flowing rhythmic lines of motion, like the feel of a drum beat, a vivid luminosity, and a style that incorporated a dance consciousness. I tried to reflect the joy of my living and traveling in Africa, especially for the young Black children here in America, who I knew were bombarded daily with negative images of our ancestral homeland. I wanted them to celebrate and feel that which came from ancient Africa, something I couldn't put into words. The noted Black historian, John Henrik Clarke, calls this our "heritage of celebration" and its roots are African. Clarke says:

> To understand the totality of our art, we must understand that we created in Africa a society where *everything* is celebrated even death as a continua-

> tion of life. Trying to capture the motion of life is
> the key to Black survival and this kind of thing runs
> through the totality of Black life. It is the ability to
> improvise within a restrictive form dictated by mood
> and circumstances.

Anyone who has heard Charlie Parker, Miles Davis, Duke Ellington, Count Basie, the world's great jazz innovators, playing their music or heard or seen James Brown or Michael Jackson sing and dance, or watched Muhammed Ali, Jim Brown, or Doctor J make their moves in the athletic sports world, knows what I mean. It is an artistic way of surviving, and this ability in itself imparts a sense of balance and a confidence to face the unknown and the difficult with renewed faith, drawing on resources unknown to us because we cannot identify them. Nonetheless, these resources belong to us and have been the basis of the art of celebration. That is, in our lives we have managed to survive oppression, not to celebrate oppression, but to celebrate survival, in spite of oppression. But the struggle is not over.

Understanding the Western Hemisphere's extreme negative and positive connotations of just the words Black and White (in that order) and all the contradictions this invokes in all of us, I would say that it is difficult for most of us to celebrate anything *all* Black...something that has been so distorted for us by racist teachings, so in most cases even the most well meaning attempts to tackle Black problems end up reaffirming the same distortion...

Seventeen years after illustrating Julius Lester's *To Be a Slave* and fourteen years after *Jambo* and *Moja* were published, the United States has moved into a new era of conservatism. Throughout the first Reagan administration certain facts kept haunting me. In this, the richest country in the world, I realized twenty-five percent of the children are on food stamps. America is eighteenth in the world in infant mortality.

My particular experiences in this country have made me extremely sensitive, not just to the things that are said but to that which is *not* said, not just to the truth that is spoken but to the truth *unspoken* or unpublished. Books as much as anything else for children in this country have to take in the reality of all the children's lives in the present as well as in the past for the children of today do affect the future. In the early eighties the blaring contradictions of our society haunted me, and since I cannot separate life from art, I needed to say something about this situation in my particular, quiet way.

Daydreamers in the very beginning was a series of individual portraits drawn from life over a twenty-year period. I held on to these drawings feeling that one day I would find some way to connect them together to tell a story.

I sent the drawings to writer Eloise Greenfield whose work I felt echoes my sentiments, and she wrote a very beautiful poem pulling all the images together spiritually. I wasn't surprised because I knew what her content would be, for we share the same vision for and about Black children. So *Daydreamers* became a book of bittersweet portraits of forty children rendered in many subtle gradations and tones on many levels. The book was meant to pull the reader in below the surface of the paper where a subdued luminous glow lingers even in the darkest faces. I sought to leave room for the subconscious to roam around slowly and freely to stimulate the viewer's deepest sense. In short, I hoped to make the reader think seriously about the lives of Black children in this country past, present, and in the future... and feeling down deep inside, that if I could get you to seriously think about the lives of the *least considered*... in this country you will think seriously about the lives of *all* the children. In this country.

So there is *Daydreamers*: and my most recent book called *Now Sheba Sings the Song* with poetry by Maya Angelou, a book that focuses on the beauty of ordinary Black women. In both books, the images, the art work came first... and was the base for the written words. Through the form of poetry, the words extended, embellished, and illuminated the art adding its own mood to these stories told through the faces of Black women and children.

But on my current work in progress the book on Slavery *The Middle Passage*... I use *art* exclusively as reading material... as text... like an extended novel.

Here the power of any words used will be completely subordinate to the emotional impact supplied by the art... for this is what I call a *picture book for adults*. The writer, Christine McDonnell, wrote these words after I showed her some of the finished art work from the book:

> Art, like literature, has the power to move beyond the limits of facts to a deeper understanding that is personal and emotional. Art jumps over our defenses, beyond the walls we have erected that protect us from pain. Art can bring us an understand-

ing that is deep and fresh. It can move _beyond the concrete limits of words._

For me...though I didn't know it when I started this project thirteen years ago...time was the essential thing I needed.

Time to tell this story, completely in pictures. The kind of time that one associates with the form of a long novel. Time for me to open myself up and experience and explore the mind not just of one single Black person going through this experience...but the minds of a _Whole People._ A people who lived and still live this slave story in all its complex social and historical disorders...right here, in America. And as time passed...as painful as it was to force myself each time, back to the drawing board...back into the agonizing past of slavery...it was equally as painful to come back through history to see the same things happening again...now...here...in the present. To see millions of hungry homeless people walking and living in the streets of our cities...while elite white collar criminals steal shamelessly millions of dollars on Wall Street in the name of Big Business and to see millions of so-called Middle and Lower class people, _Black_ and _White,_ people go on the permanent unemployed rolls. And a government that can tolerate all this...and I'm reminded of the fact that what I am looking at _is_ the result of slavery in this country. A society that tolerated the dehumanization of human beings in the past is capable of tolerating it in the present...as long as the majority of the people allow it. But all this going back and forth, coming in and out of this work, was all becoming too much for me...I personally needed _more_ insight to help me to understand all this...in order to continue to work on it. Then one day...feeling a definite need for feedback. For the first time in my life while working on any project...I decided to let my people come in and see all this work in progress. I then watched them with an artist's eyes...their faces and bodies, as they went from drawing to drawing...turning page after page...all kinds of people...young people, middle-age people, and especially _old_ people...as they all began, voluntarily to open up and tell me about their lives...and the lives of the people close to them...those who were still alive and those who had passed were now just a memory...and the people who they loved and the people they hated...and they talked about everything they knew about this country...and slavery and freedom...and freedom and slavery...and I listened.

And I began to soak up _all_ this information..._all_ these stories, _all_ these things I as one person could _never_ experience in my whole lifetime. Then when I was alone, at the drawing board...I began to let it pour out of me and use it, and let it seep slowly into all my finished paintings.

Then about seven years ago, I began to become slowly and painfully aware of the fact that a lot of time had passed and I hadn't finished this project. In working I kept doing each painting over and over until it was just right exactly right...then and only then could I move onto the next one. I seemed to have no control over the time it took to finish each piece...in fact I would *lose* all sense of time until I finished that piece.

My friends and others began to question why this project was taking me so long to complete. And some said openly to me, "We all of us...we need this book *now*...can't you see what is happening to us as a people today. We need to relive this story and gain the knowledge from our past that will sustain us in the future...please for our sake, for your sake, finish it *now*." Yes...I could see what was happening now...because my life was so thoroughly enmeshed in the past and the present that I began to doubt if I had the stamina and strength to carry that amount of responsibility on my back...to carry that added burden and still get the work done the way I wanted it done but no matter how hard I tried...I couldn't work any faster.

Then an old friend of mine...John Oliver Killens, a much older and wiser artist...a writer by profession who sometimes takes as long as fifteen years to finish a novel...John said to me:

> "Tom, don't listen to that. In our race we have a lot of 100 yard dash people...too many. But you are clearly a long-distance runner. I can't *no-one* can help you with the loneliness of that long-distance run. But I can tell you this...you will endure...because without even knowing if...for a long, long time, you have been building up...preparing yourself for this...maybe all your life. Now it's here...and you are working on it. You will endure...you will go the distance...and you will complete this work, when *you* and only you are satisfied with what you've done."

I sat down and thought about how powerful John's novels were...and all those writers and artists I respected...the ones who took the chance...to take the time...to finish their work in the only way they could in their best way...and I calmed my fears down with the realization that, though we forget sometimes that our past did not begin with chattel slavery...but in Africa, as a free people...and we sometimes lose our sense that our present is our past...and our past is our future and there is a spiritual connection that ties this all together. I *am* a story-teller and story-telling is an ancient African tradition and narrative art orchestrated painting in sequence is a natural extension of this form and is tied directly to my *particular dual heritage in this country.*

I am *blessed* to have such a powerful story to tell for this story...dealing with the vast contradictions coming out of the realities of African's and America's past experiences...the horrors of the middle passage and ironically, the affirmation of humanism...this "slave story," though a brutally agonizing story, is a beautiful saga, and the insight gained, profound, and it lends itself to depicting in art work, an extraordinary quality of energy. For by striving to overcome the distortions, false interpretations and contradictions of the past, it adds a tension that propels the best work with an incandescent power, transcending the form and allowing the viewer to get *into* the experience, living the story.

That's what the technique, the medium, the design, the drawing and the painting all of it is supposed to add up to: A Life Affirming Statement on the Quest for Human Freedom not without the raw realism of pain, but with a proper mixture of joy, balanced in such a way that at the end of the story you see, as with the life, death, and birth cycle not the end but a new beginning...A Reason for Celebration.

Finally, I believe in the ordinary, too often under-valued people. I refer to them as extraordinary, ordinary people. My own roots, as well as my heart and soul, are with these people and it is these people that I have tried to depict in my art work. I have seen the beauty, strength, and dignity in these people who we all were supposed to turn away from because of all the ugliness and pain supposedly in them. My work is thus about the masses of hard-working, poor Black people who helped build and sustain this country. I know that if you can see the joy and beauty in the blackest of us, the poorest of us past the anguish and pain of our past and present experiences and situations if you can see that, then you can feel the beauty in yourself and know your own importance and value within the human race, no matter what shape of feature or shade of color you possess.

African American Communication Tradition-Oral and Literate

Madge Gill Willis
Georgia State University

A widely held belief is that Africans and African Americans have a strong oral tradition. Although this is not untrue, the underlying assumption that usually accompanies this belief is untrue. That underlying assumption is that since Africans and African Americans have a strong oral tradition, they must not have a written tradition. This assumption is simply not true. Yet the existence of and continuing belief in this assumption should not be totally surprising given the recent unveiling that many distortions and untruths about African and African American history have been passed along as facts.

The creation of this particular myth about a non-literate African and African American communication tradition had its beginnings in non-Africans' beliefs about a connection between intelligence and literacy, and their need to create a sense of superiority.

> As literacy shapes culture, the argument goes, so it shapes human minds... More radical is the claim that mastery of a written language affects not only the content of thought but also the processes of thinking — how we classify, reason, remember. According to this view, writing systems introduce such basic changes in the way individuals think...

> Written language promotes abstract concepts, analytic reasoning, new ways of categorizing, a logical approach. (Scribner & Cole, 1981, pp. 4,5,7)

In addition, an exclusive dichotomy was created between orality and literacy.

> Oral cultures indeed produce powerful and beautiful verbal performances of high artistic and human worth, which are no longer even possible once writing has taken possession of the psyche. Nevertheless, without writing, human consciousness cannot achieve its fuller potentials, cannot produce other beautiful and powerful creations. In this sense, orality needs to produce and is destined to produce writing. Literacy...is absolutely necessary for the development not only of science but also of history, philosophy, explicative understanding of literature and of any art, and indeed for the explanation of language... itself.. (Ong, 1982, pp. 14-15)

The exaggerated claims, misinformation, and ethnocentrism in these quotes, both implied and stated, were widely believed. These theorists developed the Great Divide or Great Dichotomy theory that proposed that orality and literacy are hierarchically dichotomous and could be used to divide societies and people into preliterate, non-literate, savage and primitive versus literate, complex, modern, and domesticated (Ong, 1981; Havelock, 1963). They hailed literacy for bringing about abstract thinking, logical-empirical thought, context-independent thinking, permanent records, syllogism analysis, opportunities for reflection, and the general technologization of a society. These writers made no acknowledgment of the abundance of examples of abstract, logical reflection and analysis in oral speech nor about the existence of literacy in non-western societies.

This article attempts to correct the myths and misconceptions about the African and African American communication traditions. Then, in an historical context, some of the cognitive skills involved in orality are examined to show that cognition is abstract and advanced in oral speech as well as present in the peoples' written language. Finally, the impact of this perspective on children's literacy development is discussed with implications for teachers.

Fortunately, other (also non-African) theorists advocated a less extreme position than Ong and Havelock when confronted with the mounds of evidence that did not support such a dichotomy. Goody (1977) stated that he wanted "to maintain a balance between the refusal to admit of differences in cognitive processes or cultural developments on the one hand and extreme dualism or distinction on the other" (pp. 16-17). He saw literacy as transforming the entire societal structure including history and the types of problems and issues raised (Goody & Watt, 1968). However, Goody seemed to be having trouble maintaining his balance (Goody, 1977, p. 151) as he still claimed that there were specific qualitative cognitive differences between literate and non-literate societies in the mechanics of communication, in linguistic involvement, and in terms of problem solving skills.

Scribner and Cole (1981) similarly had difficulty letting go of their basic beliefs in the superiority of schooled literacy despite their research results. They studied the literacy of the Vai people in Liberia. The Vai teach Vai script literacy at home, and many Vai also learn Arabic and/ or English literacy in formal school situations. Scribner and Cole saw this situation as an opportunity to examine the effects of literacy with and without formal school influences. In general, they did not find a dichotomy between the literate and non-literate nor between the unschooled/ literate and schooled/literate. Results showed that literacy made only some difference on some skills. More specifically, there were no tasks on which all non-literates performed less well than all literates and, in fact, they found some non-literate persons who did as well as schooled and literate persons. As a group, however, the schooled men performed higher than non-schooled men only on tasks requiring verbal explanations. Vai script literates scored higher than others on auditory integration, rebus reading, grammar and communication games and other (seemingly) isolated skills. These results did not fit neatly into any of the researchers' theories and so they hypothesized that other factors, such as occupation, age, and living environment (urban versus rural) may be important in skill development and performance. Although no general intelligence differences were found, they considered, as Goody did, the possibility that there were undefined specific cognitive skill differences, such as memory or verbal fluency, that distinguished the literate and non-literate groups.

Scribner and Cole concluded that literacy seems to encourage the development of certain skills but that literacy is not necessary for the development of any of the skills examined (i.e., other factors also facilitated the development of these skills). They also stated that literacy along (without schooling) did not produce the same cognitive effects as schooling. The contradiction I see in these last two statements may be a result of Scribner and Cole 's minimal use of ethnography and primary use of multivariate research techniques. Although they described the uses of literacy (in all languages) and how those who were not literate in Vai script were not restricted in terms of their occupations or leadership positions, the researchers still advocate for formal schooling in order to acquire a wide range of intellectual and cognitive skills.

In trying to reach that elusive balance between relativism and dichotomization, Scribner and Cole pointed to their attempts to design some of the experimental tasks to be similar to skills and behaviors that they had observed in various natural situations. The actual functional equivalence of the experimental and real-life tasks is not clear, however, because Scribner and Cole did not evaluate it. Nor did they measure if and how their literacy-related cognitive skills were used in daily Vai life. Perhaps they should have answered those questions first.

Daniell (1987) criticized the Great Divide theorists, especially Ong. She pointed out that he gave no neurological evidence for the visual-auditory dichotomy claims he made about literacy and orality. Similarly, she found his rationalization about the memory capacity of people in oral societies to be unsupported by research evidence. Ong stated that in oral societies, there are no opportunities for advanced thinking and reflection because the people's mental capacities are exhausted in their efforts to retain the knowledge which they must commit to memory! As Daniell stated, research has found no conclusive evidence of a limit on long term memory capacity. Social and political factors in literacy were the more important ones that should be investigated, Daniell suggested.

Tannen (1982a, 1982b) took a slightly different approach to the oral-literate debate. She argued against the Great Divide because she found much overlap between oral and literate characteristics among Greek and American Jewish women (1982b). Her research refuted the context-dependent versus context-independent qualities of oral and literate communications because she found some of both in each type of language. Instead, Tannen (1982a) proposed the Cohesion Hypothesis which states that differences between spoken and written language are in how each establishes cohesion, i.e., the connections among ideas, information, relative importance,, etc. In oral speech, cohesion is created through paralinguistic attributes such as tone, pitch, rate of speaking, body language and body movement. In written speech, cohesion results from the sentence constructions, transitional phrases and specific words. In contrast to the dichotomy models that reduce and simplify language, Tannen's hypothesis offers another dimension which adds to our understanding of the complexity of language.

Heath's (1982a) classic ethnographic work, *Ways With Words,* studied the uses of language and literacy and provided further support for the idea that orality and literacy are complexly interconnected. Heath made no value judgment about the superiority of one or the other because in the African American community that she studied, orality and literacy were rarely separate and neither seemed predominant.

This latter group of researchers (Daniell, Tannen, Heath) present an informed perspective on the oral-literate question. Carrying this further, there is evidence that not only are orality and literacy intertwined in American and Greek societies, but historically, African had a literate tradition that was as much a part of the culture as the oral tradition. There actually were no "oral cultures"—there were societies where literacy, orality and various other forms of communication, such as signs, symbols and drums, were all prevalent. During African colonization and American slavery, Europeans prohibited many forms of communication as a means of oppression and control. In America, drums were forbidden and literacy for Africans was declared illegal. Although the English that was spoken by Africans in America was ridiculed, oral language became the primary means of communication for them. Hence, the focus on the oral tradition developed. Similar types of communication suppression were instituted in Africa where formal education and national business were conducted in the language of the European colonizers rather than in the languages of the African people. Yet the literate tradition was not totally destroyed.

Literacy seems to have begun with cave drawings and carvings that date back to 35,000 to 15 ,000 years B.C. in Africa and other parts of the world (Arnett, 1982). What is considered "true writing," that is, a writing script, also began in Africa (Arnett, 1982; Hilliard, Williams & Damali, 1987; Jackson, 1981; Williams, 1976) sometime before 3100 B.C. when evidence of a fully developed system was seen in ancient Kemet. (Kemet is what the ancient Egyptians called themselves and their land.) Early Kemetic writing took the form of pictograms, developed into phonograms (or syllabaries with symbols for groups of sounds), and finally incorporated alphabets (symbols for individual sounds) and cursive scripts. Writing was done in tombs, temples and pyramids, on rocks, wood, pottery, limestone, and papyrus. It was used for record-keeping, listmaking, recording songs, hymns, prayers, rituals and praises, declaring virtues of the deceased in order to help them on Judgment Day, recording history, instructing the society on how to develop character and spirituality, passing on wisdom, teaching levels of meaning, creating medical, mathematical and other scientific manuals, making school texts, recording superlative orations, transcribing court trials, and writing love poems, letters, biographies, fables, myths and religious texts (Carruthers, 1990; Hardiman, 1986; Hilliard, Williams & Damali, 1987; Simpson, 1973). A large amount of at least partially intact papyrus scrolls have been found in Kemet (Simpson, 1973; Wiedemann, 1902) which suggests that since papyrus is not indestructible, there must have been many more that did not survive the millennia. Tombs and temples are filled with writings, instructions and historical documentation. Consequently, literacy must have been widespread in order to support such a wide selection and amount of literature.

Ancient Kemetic language was called Mdw Ntr (pronounced *Medu Netcher*) by the ancient Egyptian. It literally means "word of God" and is often referred to as "Divine Speech" (Carruthers, 1990). Divine speech is both oral and written language. Greeks who studied in Kemet called the Kemetic writing system "hieroglyphics" which means "sacred letters." This spiritual nature, which was an integral part of Kemetic (and all African) life, is also reflected in the Greek word "theology" which translates literally to "divine" (theos) "speech" (logos) and also encompasses written and oral communication (Carruthers, 1990).

"Good speech" or Mdw Nfr is spoken or written speech that is grammatically correct and also virtuous or morally correct. Stating untruths or other un-godlike characteristics is not considered good speech. Karenga's (1984) translation of the Book of Amenomope illustrates: "Do not mislead a man or woman with pen and papyrus. It is an abomination to God. Do not bear witness with false words nor injure another with your tongue." (p. 61) Good speech was often enjoyed for its elegance and style. The Book of Khun Anup (sometimes referred to as the Tale of the Eloquent Peasant) and the

Book of Neferti describe how the oratory of these two men was so impressive that the kings had their words carefully transcribed into written form (Karenga, 1984; Simpson, 1973).

The importance of writing in Kemet was reflected in the high status that scribes held. They spent many years in training that involved both formal education and apprenticeships. Many young men were encouraged to pursue scribedom as a career.

> ...Set your heart/mind on books. I have watched those who are forced to toil... There is nothing better than books... I'll make you love scribedom more than your mother... It's the greatest of all callings, there is none like it in the land. (Lichtheim, 1975, p. 185)

> As for those learned scribes... their names have become everlasting even though they have departed having completed the days of their lives... Man decays; his corpse becomes dust and all his relatives die. But a book causes him to be remembered through the mouth of those who quote him. Better is a book than a well built house. (from *Song in Praise of the Learned*, Karenga, 1984, p. 84)

Writing systems developed in other parts of Africa as well. These systems included symbol systems (such as the Dogon's), syllabaries (such as the Vai script), and phonemic or alphabet systems (such as the Wolof). Others which have become known to non-African researchers (include the systems of the Ewe, Bamum, Bozos, Bambaras, Binis, Yorubas, Mende, Loma, Kpelle, Bete, N'ko, Dita, Fula, Bagam, Oberi, Okaime, and Nibidi (Klima, et al., 1976). Again, what we know of is likely only the tip of the iceberg. Undoubtedly many other groups have developed literacy systems. This abundance of writing systems provides additional evidence against the label of "restricted" literacy that Goody (1968) used.

In the 1800's, European missionaries began using the Roman alphabet to translate their religious books into African languages (Bamgbose, 1976). As missionary and colonial government schools developed, policies were made that students should be taught in the European language. Consequently, literacy in this foreign language was prioritized. The effect that these policies had on mother tongue literacy is not clear because, in practice, when the students were not sufficiently fluent in the foreign language, teachers used the mother tongue for instruction.

This method of communication suppression still exists. Not long ago many South African students died in their protests against being taught in Afrikaans, the language of the white South Africans. Currently in the United States there are heated debates going on about the legitimacy of African American language in schools that teach "standard" English. The message in this method is that the African and African American language is inferior and should be displaced. The basis for such messages is obviously not historical, linguistic, cultural nor ethnographic knowledge.

In all areas of Africa, speaking and writing were/are two aspects of the concept of The Word or Nommo. Nommo is the force that produce and influences life in the form of the Word (Jahn, 1961). The Word has power—"magical" power (Jahn, 1961; Obenga, 1989). This power comes through both the spoken word (Obenga, 1989) and the written and symbolic word (Davies, 1987; Obenga, 1989) . This magical, powerful Word has the power of creation. "It is through thought and the spoken word that Atum [God]... and all of their creations are given life... Speech, as it is used here, has a clear ontological meaning, and this ontological speech. .. calls the world into existence." (Obenga, 1989, p. 312, 315) In African creation stories, the Word of God (divine speech) is central states that "In the beginning was the Word and the Word was with God and the Word was God."

Man also can tap the power of the Word in various ways. For example, a person's word has traditionally been viewed as a reflection of his character and his honor. "His word is as good as gold" is apopularcompliment about aperson's trustworthiness and status. Anotherexample is that once a thought is expressed, it becomes real in some way. "If he said it, then it is," is a testimony to a person ' s good speech and power of authority. Jahn (1961) equates working magic with writing poetry "arranges a series of images which alter reality. . . " (p. 149) The magical power of the Word can also be seen in rituals and ceremonies where words (chants, songs, phrases, etc.) bring about certain expected results.

Heath (1985) discussed the power of the word in current African American culture, specifically in the church. Usually the focus is on the emotional and spiritual surge resulting from the power of the oral sermon. A good sermon is one that inspires and charges people. The written word is also involved in this power, usually as a stimulus in terms of the text of the sermon and the written biblical references on which the sermon is based.

Although the premise of Akinnaso's (1982) argument rests on the oral-literate dichotomy, his presentation provides evidence that African ritual (oral) communication has many parallels to written communication. Ritual communication is very different from social communication and everyday oral language in terms of its purpose, structure, and linguistic characteristics. Ritual chants, divination verses and other specific language/linguistic/interaction pattems that may involve stylized intonations and rhythms are examples of ritual communication. The specific example of Yoruba cowrie shell divination that Akinnaso uses demonstrates the power of the Word and the intertwined nature of spoken and written communication.

Given this historical background, there can be little doubt about the full range of communication traditions that have existed in Africa for at least the last 5000 years. Within this historical context, the role of orality can be understood more appropriately, as one mode of communication rather that as the *only* form. Based on this wide variety of language expressions, there also should be little doubt about the complexity of thought and cognitive functioning of Africans. However, few have attempted to describe it with the content knowledge of the entire communication tradition. Feuerstein (1979) has analyzed cognitive functions for analytical style learners and Azibo (1988) has suggested describing cognitive style using African personality traits and constructs for wholistic style learners. This is not to suggest another dichotomy, but to attempt to understand the learning process in ways that will aid teachers who work with a variety of students. The next section of this paper analyzes the cognitive skills involved in traditional African oral speech.

The meaning of cognition differs in various cultures. Carruthers (1990) described the Kemetic belief about the thinking process. Sensing or perceiving initiates knowing in the mind and then expression through speech. "Whatever the thinking process is in its own right, when one learns to speak, speech takes over the process." (p. 9) This is also evidence of the power of the word to create. To the Dogon people in Mali and Upper Volta, cognition involves levels of understanding (Griaule & Dieterlen, 1986). Information is shared in pieces and at different levels of detail. It is up to the receiver to assimilate and synthesize the knowledge, gaining increasingly deeper understandings with each round. Information is shared in an oral manner although there are visual symbols to be understood along with the spoken information. A person who has progressed through all levels or degrees of instruction is said to have achieved the "clear word'." (Griaule & Dieterlen, 1986). Egan (1987) described the "bon a' penser" or "good for thinking" characteristics of orality as several specific cognitive functions that are also seen during the oral stage of children's development. These include: memory, story form or schema, visual imagery, pragmatic thought, affective involvement, metaphoric logic and use of rhyme.

In analyzing the following oral samples, several cognition models were used: Feuerstein's (1979) twenty-seven cognitive functions, the cognitive domain part of Bloom's (1956) *Taxonomy of Educational Objectives,* the summary of characteristics of African American children's learning style described in Willis (1989), and Egan's (1987) description of thinking skills associated with orality. Samples of oral speech are from the Dogon educational process, an ancient Kemetic oration, a Liberian court case, and current African American speech.

The Dogon educational process was described above as an oral, increasingly detailed process that also involves written symbols. Cognitive skills involved include: memory of past information, awareness of similarities and contrasts among information, ability to synthesize appropriate pieces of information into an organized structure, development of hypotheses against which additional information can be checked (Feuerstein); analysis, synthesis and evaluation (Bloom); story formation or development of story schemas (Egan); and reflection (Willis).

The Book of Khun-Anup (Karenga, 1984) consists of the transcription of his good speech to the king in which he asked that justice be done in his situation:

> When you embark on the Lake of Maat may you sail on it with a good wind. May no storm tear away your sail nor your boat lag behind. May no misfortune fall on your mast and may your mainstays not snap...And may the fish come quickly to you and plump birds gather around you... A mortal man dies along with his dependents but will you be a man of eternity by your righteousness? Is it not wrong when a balance tilts, a plummet strays, and the straight becomes crooked? Lo, justice has fled from you, dri-

ven from its place... He who should set matters right makes things go wrong... Redress is short but misfortune is long and a good deed returns to those who do it... Be a shelter and make your shore safe. (pp. 31-32)

One striking aspect of this speech is the use of metaphor. The Nile River was central to Kemetic life and so water and nautical references were appropriate. Khun-Anup used nautical metaphors that were widely understood and appreciated by his cohorts. He stated the same idea in several ways using different metaphors each time. There were no direct references to his complaint, but the process of achieving justice was the focus. It was up to the listener to discern the intended meaning of the metaphors and to apply that understanding to the justice process for that specific situation. Holt (1975) described this cognitive process as an abstraction process that is inherent in the use of metaphors. Metaphors are often ambiguous by themselves, so the context in which they are used must contribute to their meaning. In addition to his use of metaphor, Khun-Anup used cognitive skills of comparison, evaluation, synthesis, logical progression, harmony, improvisation, comprehension and application.

In the African-American community, the use of metaphors is very widespread. Metaphors are seen as an expression of the African American worldview (Holt, 1975). They carry cultural information and require common understandings in order to comprehend them. As in the good speech of the ancient Egyptians, oral elegance and competence can be demonstrated through the skillful use of metaphors. Some popular examples of African American metaphors include:

Gettin' ova like a fat rat.
I don't know what page you on.
He is *out* to lunch!
Tighter than the top on a new jar of mustard.

Metaphors require the ability to handle abstract symbolism and logical analogy (Holt, 1975). Holt attributes creative or generative power to metaphors — another expression of the Word. In the following excerpts from a Kpelle (Liberian) divorce court case, PC is the "judge," Tuang is the wife, Baawei is her mother, and Baa is the husband.

PC: (to Tuang): The old lady is questioning you. She said: "Are you leaving the man because of his ways?" That is an important question she is giving you...Withcraft cannot remain on "I don't know." (A proverb meaning that a witchcraft accusation cannot be sustained by saying "I don't know" when one is pushed for justifying evidence.)

Tuang: I said that I don't want him because of his ways...

PC: (to Baawei): It reaches you. She said that she doesn't want your son-in-law any more...

Baa. (to Tuang): Are you saying that you are leaving the home because of the child's death? A palaver is just its head. (A proverb meaning that a dispute always has a single core.)...

T: I am not leaving because of the child's death. But it is my keep that you are not taking care of properly. That is what hurts me enough to make me leave you. You are behaving like that to me.

Baa: I am able to give a small explanation for what she has said.

PC: All right.

Baa: This is my wife standing so. This is my mother. It was my uncles who gave her to me.

PC: They didn't ask you about that. She said that you don't make a farm for her...(to Tuang) How long has it been since you left your father's home? How many days?

T: It has been a year and a half. My father died and I went to greet the people. Not one of Baa's people stopped there.

PC: Is that why you spent a year and a half there?

T: Not one of them came and said that she and I were to go back.

PC: We are talking a palaver. (Cole, et al., 1971, p. 179-181)

Cole et al. describe this case as a less-than-average example of debating skill in the couple. However, it demonstrates how each selectively presents information that will support his or her side and uses application and evaluation of logical argument. PC makes hypothetical arguments and comparisons of evidence presented. Many of the cognitive skills that were seen in the previous samples apply here also.

In addition, the use of proverbs brings new cognitive skills into use. Boateng (1990) tells of a Twi belief that "a wise child is talked to in proverbs." (p. 117) Not only do proverbs serve to pass on cultural traditions and beliefs, but they also provide opportunities for conceptual development (White, 1987). Similar to metaphors, proverbs have an ambiguous aspect. Verbs in proverbs are always in the present tense which suggests a timeless quality that allows them to be applied to a variety of situations. Proverbs contain a great deal of information in a few words which means that the listener must elaborate upon the meaning to gain full understanding before applying it to the situation. Often proverbs actually contain metaphors or similes and therefore involve the cognitive skills related to them. Proverbs provide common sense information and problem-solving assistance that again, must be gleaned by the listener, understood in the appropriate manner and then connected to the current situation. White describes it as "going beyond the utterance itself by using underlying assumptions to draw appropriate implications." (p. 152)

In her study of language use in White and Black communities, Heath (1982a) described the uses of spoken language (that very often were intertwined with uses of written language). African American preschool children learned storytelling skills by imitating others and then by creating their own, modifying and elaborating them based on audience feedback. They developed a storytelling schema but also showed flexibility with different types of stories and audiences. They engaged in "style shifting" to adjust their verbal and nonverbal behavior according to how they perceived and interpreted the situation.

> Track?
> Can't go to de track. dat track, to dat train track.
> Big train on de track
> Tony down by de track
> Mama git 'im
> Track, train track
> He come back. (Heath, 1982a, p. 173)

This story poem was created and recited spontaneously by a two year old. It was about an incident that had happened the day before. Although the alliteration and rhyming may not have been consciously added, its use suggests auditory matching and patterning ability as well as memory skills. All of these are appropriate skills at the two year old developmental level.

Preschoolers in Heath's study lived in an environment filled with multi-sensory stimulation. They learned to perceive the salient features for a particular task, retrieve previously gleaned synthesis skills. Heath noted that African American preschoolers were not explicitly taught any of these skills, as the common wisdom was that children come to know through learning by experience.

> He gotta learn to know 'about dis world, can't nobody tell him... Ain't no use me tellin' him: 'Learn dis, learn dat.' He just gotta learn, gotta know; he see one thing one place one time, he know how it go, see sump'n like it again, maybe it be de same, maybe it won't. He hafta try it out. If he don't he be in trouble... Gotta keep yo eyes open, gotta feel to know. (p. 84)

A characteristic that both Holt (1975) and Heath (1982a) highlight is that the ability to appropriately use metaphor develops early in African American children, however it is not included in school curricula until upper elementary grades. In fact, the children's natural tendency to link events or situations together and to create metaphors actually interferes with the standard primary grade tasks of isolating pieces and aspects of a whole (identifying shape, color, or number, for example). Heath found that for a large number of these children, by the time they had reached the upper grades where elaborations and interpretations involving comparisons of different elements were required, their earlier failures and frustrations had taken their toll. Many were turned off to the learning process and did not do well in school.

In the above examples of African American oral tradition, many of the cognitive characteristics are also found in examples of the literate tradition and in examples of European American communication traditions. This would support the position that there is no clear-cut oral-written dichotomy, that the cognitive skills involved in speaking and writing are very similar and overlap a great deal, and that a hierarchical relationship is not feasible or likely because of the interconnectedness of both forms. What seems most crucial in African communication is not how something is expressed, but that it is expressed in some meaningful form.

> From the time of Pharaonic Egypt.there have been not oral civilizations (as ethnologists and foreign anthropologists call them) but civilizations of the powerful, creative Word. Orality is but a secondary phenomenon, whether or not it can be associated with the existence of writing. (Obenga, 1989, p. 316)

So where does this leave us? I believe that it leaves us with more ways in which children can learn and come to know. The Curriculum Infusion movement that is spreading nationally promotes the dissemination of accurate and complete knowledge about Africans and African Americans throughout the school curriculum, i.e., good speech about it. Infusion takes the form of content as well as approach. The content aspect includes teaching them that there is a strong African tradition of literacy and of using words in powerful ways. The Infusion approach includes using those cultural and historical strengths, skills and perspectives that the children have in them as paths towards expanding their skills repertoire and as substance for maintaining high expectations.

Egan (1987) and Corson (1984) suggest that teachers stimulate orality. Both see strengths in the oral mode of expression and learning, and see it as an appropriate basis for developing literacy. Because both also realize that American society is an oral/literate society and not solely a literate one (probably no such society exists), both researchers also emphasize the complementary relationship between oral language, written language and various cognitive skills.

Simons and Murphy (1983) tend to focus more on the differences between spoken and written language rather than the similarities. They are concerned that children sometimes use oral language strategies in written language situations. Although Tannen (1982a, 1982b) would probably disagree with the strict tone of Simons & Murphy's characterizations, their article offers practical examples of teaching writing strategies by highlighting the differences (those that do exist) between written and oral discourse.

Heath's (1980, 1982b) suggestions involve making changes in perspective rather than just doing a different exercise or changing the emphasis. She advocates that schools become knowledgeable about the range of ways children learn, use and display their knowledge so that the school can provide opportunities for all children to have these various ways reinforced early in school. She and Frake (1983) suggest that there is a political factor that restricts literacy in our society.

In summary, this paper has documented the long history of the African and African American communication tradition, which includes a strong literate tradition as well as a strong oral tradition. Both modes of communication require a variety of advanced and complex cognitive skills and examples of these were given from African and African American literature. Finally, suggestions were given for teachers to use this awareness in the classroom with their

...ation of kids not being read to.

African American students.

The commonly given excuse that African American children have difficulty learning to read because they come from an oral (and therefore, it is assumed, illiterate) culture can no longer be used. African American children come from a communication tradition that is strong in both the oral sense and the literate sense. Any current greater emphasis on the oral aspect is due to the political and racist suppression of the written and symbolic aspects of African American culture and a refusal to acknowledge the ways in which literacy is used in the culture. Teachers must acknowledge and incorporate these ways into their instructional methods and curriculum so that they can appropriately add the "school's ways" of learning to the repertoire that the children bring.

African American children can be empowered by the knowledge that they come from a legacy of orators, singers, and musicians, as well as writers, poets and readers. Along with our oral tradition is our literate tradition—our children can excel in both.

References

Akinnaso, F. N. (1982). *The Literate Writes and the Non-literate Chants: Written Language and Ritual Communication in Sociolinguistic Perspective.* In W. Frawley (Ed.). *Linguistics and Literacy* (pp. 7-36). New York: Plenum Press.

Arnett, W. S. (1982). *The Predynastic Origin of Egyptian Hieroglyphs: Evidence for the Development of Rudimentary Forms of Hieroglyph in Upper Egypt in the Fourth Millennium B.C.* Washington, D.C.: University Press of America.

Azibo, D. (1988). *Understanding the Proper and Improper Usage of a Comparative Research Framework, Journal of Black Psychology,* Vol. 15 No. 1, pp. 81-91.

Bamgbose, A.(Ed.). (1976). *Mother Tongue Education: The West African Experience.* London: Hodder & Stoughton.

Bloom, BS.(Ed.)(1956). *Taxonomy of Educational Objectives: The Classification of Educational Goals. Handbook 1: Cognitive Domain.* New York: Long mans, Green & Co.

Boateng, F. (1990). African Traditional Education: A Tool For Intergenerational Communication. In M. K. Asante *K. W. Asante (Eds.),African Culture: The Rhythms of Unity (pp.* 109-122). Trenton, N.J.: Africa World Press. (First published 1985.)

Carruthers, J. H. (1990). *Divine Speech: The Foundation of Kemetic Wisdom.* In M. Karenga(Ed.), *Reconstructing Kemetic Culture: Papers, Perspectives, Projects* (pp. 3-23). Los Angeles: University of

Sankore Press.

Cole, M., Gay, J., Glick, J. A., & Shalp, D. W. (1971). *The Cultural Context of Learning and Thinking: An Exploration in Experimental Anthropology*. New York: Basic Books.

Cole, M. & Scribner, S. (1974). *Culture and Thought: A Psychological Introduction*. New York: J. Wiley & Sons.

Corson, D. (1984). *The Case For Oral Language in Schooling. Elementary School Journal*, 84,

Daniell, B. (1987, March). *The Uses of Literacy Theory: The Great Leap and the Rhetoric of Retreat*. Paper presented at Annual Meeting of Conference on College Composition and Communication, Atlanta, GA. (ERIC Document Reproduction Service No. ED 281197)

Davies, W. V. (1987). *Egyptian Hieroglyphs*. Berkeley: University of California Press.

Egan, K. (1987). *Literacy and the Oral Foundations of Education. Harvard Educational Review*,

Feuerstein, R. (1979). *The Dynamic Assessment of Retarded Performers*. Baltimore: University Park Press.

Frake, C. 0 (1983). Did Literacy Cause the Great Cognitive Divide? *American Ethnologist*, 10,

Goody, J. (Ed.). (1968). *Literacy in Traditional Societies*. Cambridge: Cambridge University

Goody, J. (1977). *The Domestication of the Savage Mind*. Cambridge: Cambridge University Press.

Goody, J. & Watt, I. (1968). *The Consequences of Literacy*. In J. Good, (Ed.), *Literacy in Traditional Societies*. Cambridge: Cambridge University Press.

Griaule, M. & Dieterlen, G. (1986). *The Pal Fox*. Chino Valley, AZ: The Continuum Foundation.

Hardiman, W. J. (1987) . *The Nature and Elegance of Ancient Egyptian Literature*. In M. Karenga & J. Carruthers (Eds.). *Kemet and the African Worldview: Research, Rescue and Restoration* (pp. 167-172). Los Angeles: University of Sankore Press.

Havelock, E. A. (1983). Preface to Plato. Cambridge: Belknap Press of Harvard University Press.

Heath, S. B. (1980). "The Functions and Uses of Literacy." Journal of Comrnunication, 30(1), 123-

Heath, S. B. (1982a). Ways With Words: Language, Life, and Work in Communities and Classrooms. Cambridge: Cambridge University Press.

Heath, S. B. (1982b). What No Bedtime Story Means: Narrative Skills at Home and School. Language in Society, 11, 49076.

Heath, S. B. (1985). Protean Shapes in Literacy Events: Ever-shifting

Oral and literature Traditions. In D. Tannen (Ed.), Spoken and Written Language: Exploring Orality and Literacy (pp. 91-117). Norwood, N. J.: Ablex.

Hilliard, A. G., Williams, L. & Damali, N. (1987). The Teachings of Ptahhotep: The Oldest Book in the World. Atlanta: Blackwood Press.

Holt, G. (1975). Metaphor, Black Discourse Style, and Cultural Reality. In R. L. Williams (Ed.), Ebonics: The True Language of BlackFolks (pp. 86-95). St. Louis: The Institute of Black Studies.

Jackson, D. (1981). The Story of Writing. New York: Taplinger.

Jahn, J. (19611). Muntu: The New African Culture. New York: Grove Press.

Karenga, M. (1984). Selections From the Husia: Sacred Wisdom of Ancient Egypt. Los Angeles: University of Sankore Press.

Klima, V., Ruzicka, K. F., & Zima, P. (1976). Black Africa: Literature and Language. Bingham, MA: D. Reidel.

Lichtheim, M.(1975). Ancient Egyptian Literature. Vol.I. Berkeley: UniversityofCalifornia Press.

Obenga, T. (1989). African Philosophy of the Pharaonic Period . In I. Van Sertima (Ed .)., Egypt Revisited (pp. 186-324). New Brunswick, N.J.: Transaction.

Ong, W. J. (1982). Orality and Literacy: The Technologizing of the Word. London: Methuen.

Scribner, S. & Cole, M. (1981). The Psychology of Literacy. Cambridge: Harvard University Press.

Simons, H. D. & Murphy, S. (1983, November). *Learning to Read and Write: The Influence of Oral and Written Language Differences.* Paper presented at Annual Meeting of the National Council of Teachers of English, Denver, CO (ERIC Document Reproduction Service No.: ED 248462)

Simpson, W. K. (1973). *The Literature of Ancient Egypt* (New Edition). New Haven: Yale University Press.

Steindorff, G. & Seele, K. C. (1957). *When Egypt Ruled the East* (2nd Ed.). Chicago: The University of Chicago Press.

Tannen, D. (1982a). *The Myth of Orality and Literacy.* In W. Frawley (Ed.). *Linguistics and literacy* (pp. 37-50). New York: Plenum Press.

Tannen, D. (1982b). *The Oral/Literate Continuum in Discourse.* In D. Tannen (Ed.), *Spoken and Written Language: Exploring Orality and Literacy (pp.* 1-16). Norwood, N.J.: Ablex.

White, G. M. (1987). *Proverbs and Cultural Models: An American Psychology of Problem Solving.* In D. Holland & N. Quinn (Eds.), *Cultural Models in Language and Thought.* Cambridge: Cambridge University Press.

Wiedemann, A. (1902). *Popular Literature in Ancient Egypt.* London: David Nutt.

Williams, C. (1976). *The Destruction of Black Civilization.* Chicago: Third World Press.

Willis, M. G. (1989). "Learning Styles of African American Children: A Review of the Literature and Interventions." *The Journal of Black Psychology,* 16, 47-65.

Images of African-Americans in Picture Books For Children

Judith V. Lechner, Ph.D.
Auburn University, Alabama

Because picture books send two images simultaneously, the impact they create on young children is strong and long lasting. What images can today's children find in picture books by or about African-Americans? Has the distorted mirror of the past been refinished in clear reflecting glass and silver?

For an overview and discussion of the earlier literature see Banfield (1985) and St. Clair (1989). Banfield describes the distorted stereotypes presented in nineteenth and early twentieth century books, from the contented slave on the idyllic plantation exemplified by Joel Chandler Harris' Uncle Remus, to the foolish, good natured, dishonest, and highly superstitious Black, exemplified by the cook, Dinah, who appeared in the popular *Bobbsey Twins* between 1907 and 1950 (1985 pp. 29-30)

St. Clair speaks of the early twentieth century landmarks in presenting realistic images of African-Americans in children's literature such as Charlemae Rollins' *We Build Together: A Reader's Guide to Negro Life and Literature for Elementary and High School Use.* She also describes the role in the 1960s and early 1970s of the Council on Interracial Books for Children in nurturing and bringing to public attention, through its contests, talented young African-American writers such as Walter Dean Myers and Mildred Taylor and illustrators such as Pat Cummings and Leo and Diane Dillon. For a new annotated bibliography of books by twentieth century African-Americans look for Helen E. Williams' *Books by African-American Authors and Illustrators for Children and Young Adults*, to be published by the American Library Association in 1991.

Rudine Sims covers the era between the mid 1960s and 1980s thoroughly in *Shadow and Substance* (1982). Sims developed a framework for critiquing children's literature about African-Americans, dividing the literature into three categories: socially conscious, melting pot, and culturally conscious books. Written by white writers primarily for a white audience, the socially conscious books "mean good, but they do so doggone poor." (Sims 1982, p. 29). The stories tend to be didactic, lacking in believable plot, characterization or setting, and worst of all frequently reinforcing the very stereotypes they hope to overcome. The melting pot books focus on the universal ignoring subcultural differences such as the extended family, especially the presence of grandparents, foods, and the use of Black English. (Sims, pp. 42-43).

It is the culturally conscious book that holds out the greatest promise of presenting realistic images for young audiences regardless of their own ethnic backgrounds: " A good story, well written and enriched with the specific details of living that make a cultural group distinctive, will naturally touch on the human universals extant within that cultural group. Such a story will be good literature, accessible to readers both inside and outside the group depicted."(Sims, 1982, p. 73).

Sims gives a brief biographical sketch of some of the African-American image makers who had already made a large contribution to African-American children's literature (Lucille Clifton, Eloise Greenfield, Virginia Hamilton, Sharon Bell Mathis, and Walter Dean Myers). Of these writers Clifton and Greenfield write picture books. Sims also briefly mentions several other young and promising writers and illustrators, among whom Tom and Muriel Feelings and John Steptoe have created picture books.

This article focuses on picture books from 1980 through 1991. Theme, tone, and style of text and illustrations will be discussed in an attempt to look at the images young children might receive from the books available to them in schools, public libraries, and book stores.

Warmth and reassurance characterize the general mood of most of the books under consideration. The child within the family, especially the child's special relationship with parents, siblings or grand-parents are the predominant themes in these books. Other important themes are the child in the community and African-American culture and history. The language in these books tends to be standard English with a few notable exceptions, such as Patricia McKissack's and Irene Smalls-Hector's picture books, but the vocabulary and expressions used reflect African-American style or culture. Examples include African-American names like Kyla and Tamika, referring to mother as "Mama," affectionately referring to an older child as "baby" and metaphoric language as in ".... [their Mama and Daddy missed them] like you would the sun, baby." (Johnson, in *Tell Me a Story Mama*). The majority of the picture books with African-American images published today are books of realistic fiction, written by African-American writers or illustrated by African-American artists. There are remarkably few African-American folktales in picture book format. Folktales tend to be anthologized, as in Virginia Hamilton's *The People Could Fly* (1985), and Julius Lester's *Tales of Uncle Remus: The Adventures of Brer Rabbit* (1987), though some popular picture book versions have come out recently, such as the Coretta Scott King Award winning *The Talking Eggs* by Robert D. San Souci and Jerry Pinkney, and *Jump* (1986), *Jump Again* (1987) and *Jump on Over* (1989) by Van Dyke Parks and Barry Moser. Folktales in picture book format tend to be African. African-American writers and artists active in retelling and illustrating African folktales include Ashley Bryan, Leo and Diane Dillon, Ruby Dee and Jerry Pinkney.

Very few modern fantasy stories are being written by or about African-Americans. Patricia McKissack's three books, *Flossie and the Fox* (1986), *Mirandy and Brother Wind* (1988), and *Nettie Jo's Friends* (1988); and Pat Cummings *C.L.O.U.D.S.* (1986) are the outstanding exceptions. Lucille Clifton and Eloise Greenfield's poems continue to provide the rich images of African-American children which they had already provided in the 1970s. Julia Fields adds her voice in *The Green Lion of Zion Street* (1988).

Among some of the new or continuing African-American picture book image makers (the most prolific and widely read), are the artist/writer Pat Cummings, the artist Jerry Pinkney and the writers Eloise Greenfield, Patricia McKissack and Mildred Pitt Walters. Floyd Cooper and David Soman have illustrated several books by African-American writers, including two new writers Elizabeth Fitzgerald Howard and Angela Johnson, who are likely to become even better known in the nineties. John Steptoe has died, all too young. His work will be missed.

The Child Within the Family:

Parents, siblings, aunts, uncles and grandparents are important for the age group of the intended audience, and books like Elizabeth F. Howard's *The Train to Lulu's* (1988), John Steptoe's *Baby Says* (1988) and Mildred Pitts Walter and Pat Cummings' *My Mama Needs Me* (1983) and *Two and Too Much* (1990) all deal with older siblings learning to take care of younger siblings, while Angela Johnson and James Ransome's *Do Like Kyla* (1990) presents a younger sister's admiration for her older sister.

Steptoe and Walter capture that trying time in a child's life when he or she must learn to handle the younger brother or sister who gets into everything, but is too young to be held responsible. Brandon in Walter's *Two and Too Much* has a really tough job - he must keep baby sister Gina out of trouble long enough to let Mama get ready for company. This proves to be almost more than Brandon can handle, as Gina tries to "help" by emptying the vacuum cleaner bag in the living room, as she makes herself beautiful by putting on Mama's cosmetics, and as she knocks over his "perfect three story garage." Brandon discovers how much he loves Gina in spite of his exasperation with her, when he thinks he's lost her and then finds her fast asleep on the floor next to his bed.

Steptoe's Baby is still in the crib, but he knows just how to get older brother mad with his mischievous "uh, oh" and "no, no." He keeps dropping his teddy bear out of the crib, obtaining his freedom thereby, only to wreak havoc on big brother's tower of blocks. A big wet kiss on the nose from Baby, complete with a disarming smile, soothe big brother's ire, and all is harmony as "Baby says 'Okay' !" What makes both these books unusual is their focus on the role of the older child in helping to care for the baby rather than merely having to learn to share his or her parents with the new baby. The child has an active rather than passive role.

In each of these books the illustrations present highly individualized personalities. These artists know babies in all their delightful variations, poses and actions. Cummings' illustrations for *Two and Too Much* are highly molded, with each fold in the clothes emphasized, and with all surfaces smooth and rounded. Every cornrow on Gina's head, even her button earrings, are distinct as is the design on Brandon' s sneakers and the seams on his jeans. Cummings delights in creating shape, smooth texture and saturated colors, as is evident from her recent illustrations. The homes she depicts are comfortable, middle class homes. The effect of order is so strong that even the chaos Gina creates looks aesthetically pleasing. As milk spills, for instance, it pours out as a sheet of ribbon. This plastic effect should fascinate children with its tactile appearance. As with the other artists, however, the true appeal of the illustrations is in the portrayal of real children with their varying expressions, culminating in a final scene of angelic Gina smiling in her sleep as Brandon hugs her.

Steptoe's art had undergone great change since the 1970s, when his work was more expressionistic - strong outlines filled in with purples and blues, and was influenced by African styles and motifs (Sims, p.98). In *Baby Says* Steptoe used more shading, with pastel shades of browns, pinks, yellows and violets. The use of light is an important element and subtly adds to the warmth of the atmosphere. The focus in this book is almost exclusively on the children and their actions. It is the children's expressions that really tell the story.

Two older sisters are the focus of both Howard's *The Train to Lulu's* and Johnson's *Do Like Kyla*. The point of view in the autobiographical *The Train to Lulu's is* that of older sister, Beppy. "It's a long, long ride from Boston to Baltimore. Nine hours!" And, twelve year old Beppy has to take care of her little sister Babs. Typically shifting emotions of an older sister are portrayed as she alternates between watching the time to eat their lunches (not too early, even though they are already hungry), distracting her little sister when she begins to cry, amusing her when she is bored, and sharing with her the views from the window. The long train ride ends with hugs and kisses and praise for the smart little girls as the relatives greet them in Baltimore.

The illustrator Robert Casilla's water colors focus primarily on the girls, their expressions, movements, dresses, with an occasional glimpse of the views the girls see from the train window and of the conductors in the train. The themes of love, and feelings of responsibility and competence, are portrayed both through text and illustrations. Howard continues the theme of love between sisters and introduces a special aunt who lets them try on her hats and relates the story behind each hat, in her latest book, *Aunt Flossie's Hats (And' Crabcakes Later)* 1991.

When a little sister admires her older sister she tries to imitate her. In *Do Like Kyla* the story is told from the little sister's point of view—she watches Kyla closely and does everything Kyla does, from looking in the mirror as she braids her hair and saying "beautiful" to kissing the sunbeam on the dog's head. Johnson captures the speech and mood of childhood in this, as in all her books. Ransome's paintings capture that same mood. The breakfast scene in the kitchen shows a contemporary family — both father and mother are ready to go to work at the office, though mother makes breakfast first for the girls. The main focus of the book is on the girls themselves. The scene under the table where Kyla reads to little sister defines their close relationship, their own world of childhood.

Johnson continues the theme of the youngest child admiring and being proud of her older sisters in her latest book, *One of Three*. Together with illustrator David Soman, she has created a charming portrait of three sisters who are close, and do most things together, whether sitting in front of the bakery Saturday mornings, playing hopscotch by the trash cans, or taking a ride on the subway.

In *Just Us Women (1982)* Jeannette Caines also explores the special world a close relationship can create. In this case it is between a ten or eleven year old girl, the narrator, and her sophisticated, fun-filled young aunt. This too is the story of a journey. Not confined to traveling by train and the strict instructions of parents these two "women" break out temporarily from the confines of the family's loving ties as they take a leisurely, adventure-filled car ride to North Carolina. Planning, packing, and taking off are all part of the special event. The trip's highlights include stopping at all roadside markets and buying "all the junk we like," (trying it all on too, as the pictures show), and moseying down the back roads, something they normally cannot do when the rest of the family is along. The celebration of their freedom and closeness culminates when they "turn day around" and have breakfast at night, but the book ends with the warm welcome of the family upon their return. Pat Cummings' art perfectly complements the story. Fluid lines, dynamic angles, multiple images indicating movement, textures showing wall papers and textiles and creative use of a palette limited to yellow, blue and black make for a visually intriguing view of the "two women's" journey.

The fabric of interwoven lives in a family is portrayed in several books, as in *The Patchwork Quilt (1985)* by Valerie Flournoy, *We Keep a Store* (1990) by Anne Shelby and John Ward, *Clean Your Room Harvey Moon* (1991) by Pat Cummings and in *Tell Me a Story Mama* (1988) by Angela Johnson and David Soman.

Grandma's quilt looks old and dirty to Tanya, until Grandma explains that a quilt is more than a cover, it is memories. Grandma starts a new quilt, her masterpiece, with fabric from all the family's special clothes: a party dress, well worn corduroy pants, a work shirt, an African princess' robe made for Halloween. As the quilt grows, each member of the family is drawn into the project; and when Grandma becomes too ill to work on it, Tanya and her mother continue the work till Grandma is well enough to finish it. Grandma's wisdom and love have been passed on, along with the tradition of quilt making. Jerry Pinkney's soft mosaic-like water colors bring out each individual 's feelings in this community setting rich with detail. The individuals make up this family community.

We Keep a Store is more than a story about family. It is also about community, set in a quiet, small town, where everyone knows everyone else. The narrator, a nine or ten year old girl describes her daily life as she goes with her parents to their grocery store, watches them stack, measure, calculate and most of all work and talk with their customers. The store is shown as more than a place of business. Here the little girl does her growing up, learning from her parents and from the men and women of the community. The men spend time at the store, swapping stories around the warm stove on winter evenings, and on its shady porch in the summer. The women help mother pare apples and snap beans under the shade of the apple tree. Here all the children play together in the yard till a grown-up calls them in for the night. The illustrations too show warm portraits of mother, father and little girl deeply entwined in a traditional community, close to each other and their neighbors.

A very different picture is presented in *Clean Your Room Harvey Moon*. Harvey is surrounded by all the material trappings (games, books, T.V., high-tech toys such as a robot, and clothes spilling out of drawers) which modern society has to offer. Harvey's room is a mess. This allows Ms. Cummings to display a riot of objects in the most saturated of bright colors and dynamic juxtaposition of shapes. In humorous verse she describes what is perfectly obvious even to a preliterate child, the delightfully engrossing mess in Harvey Moon's room. Mother's reminders to clean up the mess vaguely filter through to this den of delights, till the final reckoning, when she inspects the "cleaned up" room and starts Harvey on the job of really cleaning up.

Tell Me a Story Mama acts as a bridge between the worlds of traditional small town life and contemporary life. A little girl asks her mother to tell a story. The story Mama tells has been told many times before, about her childhood in the country during the

Depression, of everyday joys and fears, and most of all of her parents' love. The little girl asks a question: "Why did Grandmama and Grandaddy send you and Aunt Jesse off to St. Louis when you were both younger than me? Alone, on a train?" The answer to this question, which is so important to all children who have ever had a similar experience, is reassuring: "They had to work, and your great-aunt Rosetta was lonely for children.." But their Mama and Daddy missed them "...like you would the sun, baby."

The image of children with grandparents is an especially popular and affecting one. Grandparents are shown in many different roles, from sole care giver in *Grandmama's Joy* (1980) by Eloise Greenfield and Carole Byard, companion in Angela Johnson and David Soman's *When I am Old With You* (1991), to wise counselor in both Grand Pa's Face(1988) by Eloise Greenfield and Floyd Cooper, and in A Visit to the *Country (1989) by* Herschel Johnson and Romare Bearden.

In most of the stories discussed earlier, the children live in comfortable middle class homes, though some may have more money to spend than others. In *Grandmama's Joy* comfort is conveyed through Rhondy's comments about the things she loves about her home and through the illustrations by the presence of house plants, tea cup and honey on the table, but we know money is scarce. Being too poor to be able to afford the new, higher rent for their apartment, Grandmama becomes despondent as she gets ready to leave their home and neighborhood, until Rhondy (Grandmama's joy) reminds her that what matters is that they are together. Byard's brown charcoal illustrations can be both somber and warmly reassuring by turns, as the mood of the story shifts.

Grandfather and grandson have a lighthearted, companionable time together in a world of their own, far from the pressures of time and jobs. Told from a young child's point of view, life with grandpa means sitting in a rocking chair and "talking about everything," it means sitting underneath an old tree by the road and playing cards all day, waving to the cars that go by, talking to the people they meet as they go walking, and at the end of a long walk, sitting in a rocking chair (with Grandpa napping). Soman's illustrations make this a touching vignette of the ties that can be especially strong between grandparents and grandchildren in a timeless world of being. This is a nostalgic book of a time that perhaps never was, yet the mood of love and peacefulness conveyed by both text and illustration make the reader want to believe in it.

Fear and tension are natural to childhood even in the most stable, and loving homes. Greenfield depicts the fears a child experiences when she sees an unexpected side of her actor grandfather, and believes his pretend-ugly face might some time be turned on her. Her true fear, of course, is of losing his love, but it is Grandpa himself who reassures her of the constancy of his love for her. Floyd Cooper's illustrations present a many-faceted image of Grandpa as his expressions change from merry to loving to mean to concerned and to relaxed and friendly.

Illustrations for children have been, for the most part, representational. In the last ten years illustrations have become more detailed and more elaborately painted than ever. This general rule is also true for books by African-American artists. One striking exception to this rule is Romare Bearden's illustrations for A *Visit to the Country*. Executed by Bearden just one year before his death, this is his parting gift to children, a vision of the rural South as he remembered it, in an explosion of colors and expressive images which are more important for the emotions they convey through swirling lines, than for realistic shapes or details. The story describes a boy's visit to his grandparents' farm, where he not only learns to do the chores, but learns that loving someone, in this case a red-bird that he had saved, means also giving it its freedom when it is ready to fly. His grandparents' gentle, understated advice helps him grow in understanding.

The Child in the Community

For many African-American children the concrete sidewalk, the crowded city neighborhood, the sounds that come from nearby apartments are far more familiar than the sights and sounds of a small-town grocery or the birds of the South. Irene, in *Irene and the Big Fine Nickel* (1991) by Irene Smalls-Hector and Tyrone Geeter, lives in Harlem. She has an eventful Saturday, though it starts out slowly enough "Okay, brown toes, time to wake up..." The author describes a low income house where Irene has to share a bed with her sisters and brother, and where the toilet is in a public hallway which she passes on the way to her friends' apartment, to see if their mother, Miss Sally, had started making banana pudding yet. In the course of the day Irene is seen doing dance movements to play songs like "Down, down baby, down the roller coaster..." with her Southern friend Charlene. They pass the grocery store and a record store where they hear a James Brown record and play a hand game to its words.

When the children begin to play a teasing game, Charlene becomes offended and angry, and they end up almost getting into a real fight. Irene runs home to get ready for the fight by putting Vaseline on her arms, face, and neck, so she would be more slippery. When Charlene disappears instead, Irene remembers that her grandmother always tells her "ladies don 't fight, unless they have to." The day ends in harmony when Irene finds a nickel and she shares the raisin bun she gets with it with her friends, including Charlene, who has returned. Irene recalls her grandmother's words as she decides to share with Charlene: "God don't love ugly, bein' mean and fightin' is not the best thing to do."

The sounds and sights of the city street are captured in the text and Tyrone Geeter' s paintings add the details the text omits, such as Irene's posters in her room, the signs on the store windows, the girls ' movements as they play "Down, down baby," and the bakery owner' s beautiful African headdress. In this book, even though its setting is a poor urban neighborhood, emphasis is on the positive, the network of friendships and caring adults in the neighborhood who watch out for the children.

The Child in Touch With the Past
In the late 1960s and 1970s several writers evoked the spiritual ties with Africa from African-American children in picture books such as Clifton's *All Us Come Cross the Water* (1973) and Greenfield's *Africa Dream* (1977). In the 1980s and 1990s the emphasis seems to have shifted away from making such direct connections. While African folktales have been retold and illustrated in picture books, direct historical allusions for the youngest audiences refer to images of a more recent past of one or two generations ago, in the U.S.

Elizabeth F. Howard described life in turn of the century Baltimore for Chita, the daughter of a physician, as she and her family get ready for Christmas, in *Chita Christmas Tree.* The illustrations by Floyd Cooper provide the exact time of the setting, the text merely suggests an earlier time, when physicians made their rounds in horse-drawn carriages. As Chita and Papa ride out to the country to pick Chita's own Christmas tree, they pass the red and green decorated downtown shops on Druid Hill, and the George Washington Monument, buying hot sugary waffles from the waffle man. Christmas dinner is a blend of traditional Southern and Northern feasts: creamed oysters, Smithfield ham, chestnuts, hominy, sauerkraut, candied sweet potatoes and Aunt Grace' s prize plum pudding. Dinner is followed by dancing, with music played on the parlor piano.

Ragtime Tumpie (1989) by Alan Schroeder is a fictional account of singer/dancer Josephine Baker's childhood in St. Louis. Tumpie's love of music and dancing is the predominant theme, but interwoven in the story are references to collecting fallen coals from the train and fallen fruit from the fruit stands to stretch the family budget, to the medicine man with his patent medicines, and to the world of honky tonk music and musicians. The paintings by Bernie Fuchs depict early twentieth century St. Louis street scenes, horse drawn wagons and clothes. In an afterward the author explains that Tumpie grew up to be Josephine Baker, and provides a brief biographical sketch.

One of the very few fantasy stories by or about Afro-Americans, *Mirandy and Brother Wind* (1988) by Pat McKissack and Jerry Pinkney, provides a vivid picture of country life at the turn of the century. Inspired by a photograph and stories about Ms. McKissack's grandparents, the story describes Mirandy as she gets ready for the cakewalk contest that she is determined to win. Following the advice of her elders, she manages to catch Brother Wind with whose help she and her friend, Ezel, win the contest. Customs, clothes, African-American dialect, and scenes of people working and going to church bring children into touch with the past in a light yet authentic manner.

For a long time, no stories set during the time of slavery had been told for younger children by African-Americans (Joyce Hansen's *Which Way Freedom* (1986) is for older children), because young children have no sense of historical perspective and might see only the helplessness of African-Americans as slaves, rather than the strengths they showed in keeping their spirits alive even under such terrible circumstances. In the *Ballad of Belle Dorcas* (1990) William Hooks has retold and Brian Pinkney has illustrated a North Carolina coastal legend set in slave times. As with many ballads, the emphasis is on steadfast love and heroic sacrifices to save or keep a lover. Belle Dorcas' husband, Joshua, is about to be sold away from the plantation, and in order to be able to keep him Belle goes to a conjure woman for a spell. The cruelty of life on the plantation is very apparent from the story, giving the legend a realistic setting. But, though a picture book, and a well told story, it seems more appropriate for older children, who distinguish between the folk/magical elements of the legend and realistic solutions to great problems.

Images of Real People:
Few biographies have been written for the young. Biographies of African-Americans by Eloise Greenfield, James Haskins and Patricia McKissack are for older children, though McKissack has written a younger children's biography, *Our Martin Luther King* (1986). The emphasis in this book, however, is on how the children in a first or second grade class celebrate Martin Luther King's birthday. Only a few factual details are given about Martin Luther King's life and the Civil Rights movement. A more detailed picture book biography by Irvin Adler and Robert Casilla is *A Picture Book of Martin Luther King. Jr.* (1989). The facts are given on a level even a young child can understand, and the water colors present good likenesses of Dr. King, Mrs. Coretta Scott King, Rosa Parks and historical figures who had inspired Dr. King, such as Frederick Douglass, Harriet Tubman and George Washington Carver. The illustrations accurately depict some of the events of the Civil Rights Movement, including the scene of Martin Luther King giving his "I Have a Dream" speech at the 1963 March on Washington.

Adversity breeds heroes and African-Americans have a great many heroes whose courage, perseverance and idealism can serve as inspiration for the young. The collective biography, *Afro Bets:Book of Black Heroes from A to Z* (1988) by Wade Hudson and Valerie Wilson Wesley, includes fifty African-American and African heroes— from Ira Aldridge the nineteenth century actor, to Shaka, King of the Zulus. The brief biographical sketches, accompanied by portraits of each person, are concise, but highlight the person and the circumstances that evoked the hero in him or her.

Images in Fantasy:
Fantasy tends to be allegorical, futuristic. Sims noted in 1982 that African-Americans rarely feature in modern fantasy stories (Sims, p. 106). This is still true today. *C.L.O.U.D.S.* by Pat Cummings is an unusual and delightful exception. "Chuku had just come to work at the department of Creative Lights, Opticals and Unusual Designs in the Sky." Thus began Chukus, the young sky designer's training and sky painting adventures. He is told the basic rules, and told to keep his designs simple at first. His first assignment is New York City. The only advantage to this assignment is that "Nobody ever looks up! " After a while he discovers that some people, a little girl in particular, do look up, and that he can bring joy to their lives by painting the sky with special cloud designs. When he is told that he

is to be transferred, because of his excellent work, to a more rewarding site in the tropics, he finds that he is sorry to have to leave. Chuku is shown as resourceful, creative and caring.

Children in Poetry:

Everett Anderson's Goodbye (1983) by Lucille Clifton and Ann Grifalconi seems to be the last in the Everett Anderson series. Each of the books in this series deals with five year old Everett' s feelings in different situations. In this book the poetry is very personal, lyrical. Everett's father had died and Everett goes through the five stages of grief, to final acceptance: "Everett Anderson says, 'I knew/ my daddy loved me through and through, / and whatever happens when people die / love does not stop, and/ neither will I.'"

For the very youngest "readers" Cheryl Hudson's and Bernette Ford's rhymes, and George Ford's illustrations in *Bright Eyes, Brown Skin* (1990) provide images of nursery school children playing. "Bright eyes, Brown skin.../A heart shaped face A dimpled chin..."

Julia Fields' *The Green Lion on Zion Street* (1988), illustrated by Jerry Pinkney, is a "thriller" story poem. The children wait for the bus in the fog and get the shivers as they watch a green lion on the street in the mist. Overcoming their fears they explore and confirm for the hundredth time that this is a magnificent stone lion. Use of repetition and colorful expressions make the poem suspenseful and satisfying for reading aloud. "If you just whisper 'Boo...'/ they will burn that foggy bottom dry./ Want to know why?/ Want to know why?./

'cause when they cross that bridge,
When they cross that bridge,
   on that ridge, they are going to see something crouched
up there, lolled up there
to give anybody a scare.
    It will raise their hair.
        Brave or not.
It will raise their natural hair.
See,
    that is where they will meet the lion.

Green, green lion.
   Fierce.
      Mighty.

Proud

Fierce.

Smirky.

Vain."

I have left Eloise Greenfield's Nathaniel *Talking (1988)*, illustrated by Jan Spivey Gilchrist for last, as the culmination of all the ideals expressed by Greenfield herself and by others such as Sims of what should constitute good literature by and about African-Americans. Greenfield tries to sustain children's interest by:

> (1) Giving them a love of the arts, (2) encouraging them to hold positive attitudes towards themselves, (3) presenting them with alternative methods for coping with the negative aspects of their lives, (4) giving them an appreciation for the contributions of their elders, (5) providing true knowledge of Black (African and American) heritage, (6) allowing them to fall in love with Black heroes, (7) reflecting and reinforcing positive aspects of their lives, and (8) sharing her own love of words (Sims, 1982, p. 83). In *Nathaniel Talking*, Greenfield does all of the above.

Nathaniel is nine (we know because he tells us), and lives with his father and grandmother. His mother had died. Nathaniel tells us how he feels about his family and friends, about missing his mama and how he remembers her, how he made his first friend in school, and how he feels when he misbehaves. Each topic or reminiscence is told in a different style of poetry, starting and ending with Nathaniel's rap. When he tells how his grandmother used to play the "bones" as a young woman in the 1940s and still plays it for him sometimes, we hear two different types of poems, Nathaniel's free verse and the rhythmic onomatopoeia of the clackety clack of the bones. In *My Daddy* Nathaniel uses the blues to describe how his daddy plays the blues on his guitar. At the end of the book Greenfield inserts a historical note about playing the bones, and introduces a method of counting the beats in a blues poem so that children can get the right feel for the rhythm of the blues .

The best way to get a feel for this joyful book, however, is to read it in its entirety, as it is all of the poems as a group that gives the reader the full auditory, emotional, and visual enjoyment.

Conclusion:

The last ten years have been a time of bringing to fruition many of the precepts of African American writers, artists and scholars about what children's literature by and about African Americans should be. Writers and artists already active in the seventies have continued to produce picture books that are nourishing to children, especially to African-American children who have had so few opportunities to see their lives reflected in picture books. New writers and artists have emerged and have been widely recognized for the literary and artistic images they have brought to all American children.

Not all the news is good, however. While a few African-American writers and artists have become widely recognized, overall the proportion of books produced by African-Americans is no greater today than it was ten years ago. In the mid 1980s there was a drop in the number of books created by African-Americans. Since 1986 the proportion of books by African-Americans is 1% each year. For the 1990 Coretta Scott King Award fifty-one (51) nominees were submitted out of that year's 5000 published books . In 1989 eighteen (18) of the forty-nine (49) books by African Americans had been published by small presses rather than large publishers (Kathleen Horning, 1991). All of this suggests that in spite of the many talented African-American writers and artists, publishers believe there is not a large market for stories with African-American protagonists. Yet, a well told story, with believable characters is a story for everyone. Further, it is especially important in picture books to have all segments of society well represented through authentic stories, as these are the books teachers, librarians and family members read to children. These are the stories that show children their world and that help them understand their world. The books discussed in this article help children do that, but more such books are still needed.

Works Cited

Banfield, Beryle. "Racism in Children's Books: An Afro-American Perspective." reprinted in *The Black American in Books for Children: Readings in Racism.* 2nd ed. Edited by Donna Rae MacCann and Gloria Woodard. Scarecrow, 1985. pp. 23-38.

Horning, Kathleen. Introduction to "Publishing Multicultural Books for Children and Young Adults in the 1990s," a conference session at the American Library Association 110th Annual Conference. Atlanta, June 29-July 4, 1991.

My Calling as a Storyteller

Cynthia Watts
Atlanta Based Storyteller

My earliest memories are of hearing the lyrical voices of my people. I've always loved to hear people talk — the rhythm, cadences, inflections, enuciations — all are special.

I grew up in Philadelphia, but my development was tempered by my Virginia heritage. My grandmother, Mary Woodson Ogburn Boyd, along with my parents Gilbert and Artice Watts were my primary care givers. Each spoke differently I was most intrigued with my grandmother's language. Lyrically soft, full of expressions that only she could use correctly. I was captivated by her speech, but I learned early that my grandmother 's speech was not appropriate for me in school.

As a child I traveled with my grandmother to visit Virginia her home place. In the quiet, peacefulness of rural Virginia I heard stories. I heard background information on all the people I might later meet as well as people who had gone before me. My great-great-grandmother was always referred to as "the ole white woman what live on the hill." My great aunt, who loved only one man, and when denied permission by her father to marry him, became somewhat of a recluse, died a virgin in her mid sixties. My paternal grandfather left his home and the cows roaming the field and began walking to Philadelphia to join his children out of his own loneliness. Such stories helped me under stand the family of which I am a part.

But in addition to family stories I also learned of Fox and the grapes, and grasshopper and ant. Later I found these stories told to me by my grandmother were the classical *Aesops Fables*. Perhaps because I learned them at grandmother's knee, I like animal tales best. They are non-judgemental, non-threatening and teach moral lessons. My grandmother taught me this way and I think I am a better person because of it. But how did a woman who was schooled only to the 4th grade know these stories? She came to know them in the same way as I know about family and customs and cultural practices the oral tradition.

The third week of August was revival in the church founded by my great grandfather, Starlight Baptist Church. It was there on long, hot, suffocating evenings I heard the cadence and rhythms of powerful Black preachers. And such wonderful singing. My grandmother and two of her sisters were usually there along with younger family members who lead the opening of prayer service with song and prayer. The repeated phrases of these prayers are indelibly stamped in my mind. Opening with "Dear Mother and Father God, teach me how to pray and what to pray for" and concluding with "Lord when I have run the last mile of the journey, may the guardian angel cry out well done thy good and faithful servant, thou hath have faithful over a few little things, I will make thee ruler over many." These experiences and the beauty of the language are always with me.

As a child my vivid imagination developed my verbal skills through creating and telling stories to my family, around campfires at summer camp and to some degree in school. Much later, after attending college and becoming and academician, my writing skills surfaced as a theater critic, newsletter editor and radio talk show host. I also engaged myself in community theater as an actress and public relations person.

However, my true calling came in the performance of storytelling. It is through my own storytelling that I continue to hear and sometimes share the rhyme and cadence of Black English. Our language is beautiful, if inappropriate in some settings. Through my sharing of stories I want the audience to hear and enjoy as I do. Is it possible that any one not find humor, enjoyment and understand political intent through the work of Paul Lawrence Dunbar or Langston Hughs' Jesse B. Simple?

While I enjoy performing and sharing stories I have the opportunity to see how stories change people. It is said that storytelling is at the heart of the human experience. I see this humanness in all audiences. Sometimes, at first, there is doubt that anything so simple as having a person talk could be so involving. Next the faces of audience members relax they are involved. Before performing at a juvenile detention center, I was cautioned that there might be some disruptive behavior from the teenagers. They were in the facility from crimes ranging from car theft to prostitution and drugs. My audience was seated slumped in chairs and avoided eye contact, but once I began to speak they began to change. Soon after beginning, there was laughter, some audience participation and their faces opened. I could see them as the children they were.

The benefits of storytelling are many, not only does the art form share culture and history, it is a foundation of many educational pursuits. Children seemingly love to listen to stories. As they do so they are developing skills; organizing ideas, learning vocabulary, acknowledging points of view, appreciating world view and aural/oral language skills. In workshops with teachers it takes only gentle proding for them to acknowledge what experience has taught. Children love and learn from stories.

The Pied Piper of Isleford: Ashley Bryan

Kemie Nix
Executive Director
Children's Literature for Children
Atlanta, Georgia

On the small island of Isleford off the coast of Maine, the author and illustrator of children's books, Ashley Bryan, makes his home. This unique artist is genuinely fond of children, and they return his affection. The young islanders, including the seasonal summer visitors, tag after Ashley so frequently that he is known locally as *The Pied Piper of Isleford.*

Although this Pied Piper does play a mean pipe, a wooden recorder, his clothing is neither pied nor bright. Fond of casual clothes in earth tones he saves bright colors for his books and paintings. Tall and lean with smooth brown skin, Ashley has a distinctive look. His long face is framed by his grey mustache, sideburns, and hair brushed back from a high forehead. His face is open and readable, readily showing his emotions through his black, active eyebrows, dark, expressive eyes, and highly mobile mouth. His hands are those of an artist, slender with long fingers. While he confesses that he is innately shy, his demeanor is warm and approachable.

Living on a small island suits Ashley, who has never learned to drive. He can work in his studio, paint in his garden, beachcomb along the shore, do his errands and visit his friends all without getting into a car. His lifestyle seems quite enviable until one considers the frenetic pace he keeps up when he leaves the island. In great demand as a speaker at conventions, conferences, colleges, and schools, Ashley goes on frequent speaking tours that keep him away from Isleford for months at a time. Now Art Professor Emeritus of Dartmouth College, for many years his teaching schedule also kept him away from his beloved island (to which he moved from the Bronx over two decades ago).

Born in Harlem on July 13, 1923, Ashley grew up in the Bronx in New York City during the thirties. He was the second child of six, but his parents, who moved to the United States from Antigua in the West Indies after the First World War, took in so many young relatives and friends that Ashley considers his family to be large and extended. Accustomed to calling his parents' friends, "aunt" and "uncle," boundaries between friends and relatives seemed and continue to seem irrelevant.

The apartments in which Ashley's family lived were always filled with music, plants, flowers, birds, and neighborhood children who were attracted by his parents and the atmosphere they created. Although Ashley's father made only a modest living as a printer, he was unable to resist buying birds. The living rooms of the various apartments in which they lived were lined with shelves filled with bird cages. Once young Ashley counted over a hundred birds in his home. His mother sang so constantly that his father used to say, "Son, your mother must think she's a bird." In return, Ashley's mother was fond of saying, "If I want any attention around here, I'd have to get in a cage."

Shy, introspective, and an inveterate painter and drawer from earliest childhood, Ashley was always happiest at home with his mother and art supplies. Once when he went on an overnight visit to the home of friends, when bedtime arrived, he began to cry, "I want to go home; I want to go home." To his immense relief, he was kindly returned to the bosom of his family.

By the time Ashley was fifteen, he had not only decided on a career as an artist, he had assembled a portfolio. Applying for admission to an art school, Ashley said that this portfolio was praised very highly by the admissions committee. He was told that it was the best portfolio they had seen, "but it would be a waste to give a scholarship to a 'colored person,' because there is no place for you in the field." Refusing to give up, he took a practical exam for admission to Cooper Union Art School in which a student's work was submitted anonymously. Ashley's talent spoke for itself, and he attended Cooper Union Art School on scholarship after graduating from high school.

Events conspired to keep him in the Bronx during most of his adult life. When one of his two younger sisters, Emerald, lost her husband while she was pregnant with her fourth child, he stepped in and became the father figure for her children. Without ever marrying himself, Ashley spent the next eighteen years embroiled in the myriad details of raising four active children in addition to continuing to work in his studio. It wasn't until Emerald's youngest child reached eighteen that Ashley allowed himself to aspire to the quiet lifestyle to be found on a small island.

From kindergarten, where his teacher taught him to bind his work into one-of-a-kind books, Ashley became a confirmed bookmaker. Almost forty years later, Jean Karl, the founder and editor of the children's book department at Atheneum, was brought to his studio in the Bronx. After seeing his handmade books, as well as his paintings, she asked him to do a children's book for Atheneum. A quarter of a century and a dozen books later, Ashley is still publishing with Atheneum.

His very first book for children (an ALA Notable Book), *The Ox of the Wonderful Horns,* is a collection of African folktales. This book was followed in later years by two companion volumes of African folktales. *Beat the Story Drum, Pum Pum* was also an ALA Notable Book and won the Coretta Scott King Award for the Best Illustrated Book of 1980. *Lion and the Ostrich Chicks* was a Coretta Scott King Honor Book of 1986. All three books are illustrated with block prints. Most are black-and-white half or three-quarter page prints, but some are full-page tri-colored prints. All the prints are bold, subtly humorous, and have the curving, flowing lines that are distinctive of Ashley Bryan. He is also fond of angles and many find their way into his work no matter what the medium.

Despite being an essential homebody, Ashley has traveled extensively in Europe and Africa. (He first visited Europe as an American G.I. during World War II. At that time, black enlisted men served together in companies under white officers. Ashley's company was set to work loading and unloading ships in France.) Everywhere that he has traveled, he has discovered that people love to sing the African-American spirituals. Rooted in the ordeal of slavery and developed from the African musical culture, the spirituals are African-

America's most distinctive contribution to the world of music. When Ashley realized that no one had every published these spirituals for children, although over a thousand have been collected since the Civil War, he decided to do so. He has published two volumes, *Walk Together Children: Black American Spirituals* and *I'm Going to Sing: Black American Spirituals vol. II*, both ALA Notable Books. Each double-page spread has a black-on-white, emotionally expressive block-print (reminiscent of woodcuts) on the right-hand page with the music and words on the left. The music and words have also have cut out by Ashley (a task rendered infinitely more difficult as every note and letter must be cut out backwards).

His third collection of spirituals, *All Night, All Day, A Child's First Book of African-American Spirituals*, was illustrated in an entirely different style, as were his illustrations to accompany the spirituals collected by his friend and colleague, John Langstaff - *What a Morning! The Christmas Story in Black Spirituals* and *Climbing Jacob's Ladder: Heros of the Bible in African-American Spirituals*. All three have been illustrated in the brightest of watercolors with yellows, golds, tans, and oranges predominating. In these beautifully rendered paintings, Bryan's distinctive curving lines generally draw the viewer's eyes "heavenward." It is also refreshing to see angels, heroes of the Bible, and even the Baby Jesus depicted as black. This will have a positive impact upon children black or white.

The illustrations to *Turtle Knows Your Name*, a folktale from the West Indies, are also rendered in flowing watercolors. For *The Dancing Granny*, however, Bryan utilizes black sketches against a gray background to capture Grnany's movements as she dances across pages. In *The Cat's Purr*, a perfect small book, the sketches of Caat and Rat are drawn ina warm cinnamon.

Ashley is a gifted writer as well as illustrator. *Sh-Ko and His Eight Wicked Brothers* is a Japanese folktale which Ashley retold but did not illustrate (it was illustrated by Furrio Yoshimura). It shares a common attribute with all of his stories; they all read aloud extremely well. Firmly grounded in the poetry, music, and oral traditions of African-Americans (by way of the West Indies), his words capture not only spoken language but also sounds such as a Jackal's cries, a frog's croak, or a cat's purr.

It delights all of his audiences (and I have been fortunate enough to be in many) to hear Ashley retell some of his own stories. He uses his voice as an instrument to captivate his listeners. It does. Awash in talent, Ashley Bryan is indeed a Pied Piper. His audiences are eager to follow his imagination anywhere.

References

A. Bryan, *Ashley Bryan Brochure*, Atheneum, 1985, pg. 2.

A. Bryan, *Ashley Bryan: Portrait of a Storyteller*, National Geographic Explorer, National Geographic Films, Feb., 1988.

A. Bryan, "A Tender Bridge," *Journal of Youth Services in Libraries*, Vol. 3, No. 4, Summer 1990, p. 301.

African-American Women Writers of Adolescent Literature

Rosalie Black Kiah, Ph.D.
Norfolk State University, Virginia

African-American writers have been on the scene almost as long as any other American writers. African-American women writers were among the early authors of published slave narratives and autobiographical accounts. Those unable to write their own accounts told their stories to those who could. Phyllis Wheatley was taught to read and write by her slave owner and consequently in 1770 she became the first slave and only the second woman during that period to publish a book of verse in America.

The 1920's and 1930's witnessed a revival of awareness and self-esteem by African-American writers and poets. These decades were known as the "Harlem Renaissance," and accordingly brought forth an upsurge of African-American creative expression combined with an increased public awareness of African-American talent and artistry. The writings of this era gave expression to the frustrations and joys of a people long held in bondage. The "Harlem Renaissance" gave us such writers as Zora Neale Hurston, Georgia Douglas Johnson and Jessie Redmond Fauset who through their sense of independence and racial pride, encouraged their readers to draw their own conclusions.

In the 1940's and 1950's the writings of Gwendolyn Brooks and Margaret Walker Alexander began to appear. Similarly, many new African-American writers emerged in the 1960's; among these were a number of African-American women who were encouraged in part by the Civil Rights Movement. These writers dealt with the African-American experience as it manifested itself in the human conditionwith being poor, frustrated, weak, old and sad, as well as being young, happy heroic and in love.

In the context of the Civil Rights movement, educators came to discover that much of the materials they were using presented a distorted portrait of African Americans - or simply failed to mention them at all. It became apparent that many books did not deliver images upon which African-American children could build and expand their own worlds; likewise, these books for young readers seemed to foster prejudice by planting false images in the minds of children both Black and White.

The mission then of the African-American writers of the 1960's was to provide young African-Americans with literature that was true, appropriate and relevant. The timing seemed just right. By 1964, the Civil Rights Act had been passed and the nation's consciousness had been penetrated.

The publishing houses were ecstatic as they followed the market. Their primary concern, of course, was sales. Hence there was a deluge of books about Black people flooding the market and while the quantity increased, the quality did not. With this came the problem of accuracy and authenticity of portrayals of the group, or more aptly put, the treatment of African-American in literature for children and adolescents.

Since this problem did exist, considerable attention had to be given to the credentials of writers who sought to simulate the African-American experience in their stories. Judith Thompson and Gloria Woodard commented on this in an article entitled, "Black Perspective in Books for Children," when they stated that the credentials of the writer who undertakes a book about Blacks must include a Black perspective based on an appreciation of the Black experience." It was deemed imperative then, that there be writers who could authentically present the African-American experience rather than simply presenting the issues or merely commenting on them.

These writers were needed to provide suitable materials for children as well as adolescents. It was essential that this be done because research has revealed that from the earliest school entry through graduation from high school, the child (and in this instance, the

African-American child) needs continued opportunities to see himself/herself and his/her racial group portrayed in a realistic and positive light. But where were these writers to be found?

The most obvious answer to this question would be to look from within. Careful scrutiny revealed that there was a cadre of African-American women whose credentials were more than adequate. Others were involved in writing fiction for adolescents by entering contests such as those sponsored by the Council on Interracial Books for Children in the late 1960's. Sharon Bell Mathis and Kristen Hunter are two writers who began this way. This contest was undertaken to mock the accusations that African-American writers would not or could not write well enough to be published and if published would only reach a small market. However, the success of those who entered the contest and won has demonstrated that not only were they excellent writers but that their work did have viable markets. These were writers who were excited about the opportunity to chronicle their own experiences.

Others got their opportunity through inside contacts with people who worked for publishing houses or through publishers who were willing to take a chance. Whatever the case may be, by the mid-to-late sixties and seventies, African-American women writers of adolescent literature were coming into their own. These women reflected their blackness in their writing together with reflections on the universal experience.

As best can be determined, there are approximately 15 African-American women who write adolescent literature. This list is by no means restricted to these 15 women but they represent a substantial number of known female writers of color who write adolescent literature. Some of these write for children and adolescents while some write exclusively for adolescents. The names of these writers may be familiar to many because they have written a number of novels, but also included on this list are women who have a single novel to their credit. Absent from this list are names of women who write primarily for adults but who are read by adolescents. Our list of writers include: Alice Childress, June Jordan, Eloise Greenfield, Sharon Bell Mathis, Nikki Grimes, Dindga McCannon, Rosa Guy, Ellease Southerland, Virginia Hamilton, Mildred Taylor, Joyce Hansen, Joyce Carol Thomas, Kristen Hunter, Mildred Pitts Walter, and Brenda Wilkinson.

In characterizing the literature written by these authors, it would be safe to say that the African-American experience is basically reflected in their writings. There are several components that comprise the African-American experience and these have been found in whole or in part in just about all of the offerings of the writers on this list. The components include: *The Patrimony of Africa, The Patrimony of Domination and Dependency,* and *The Patrimony of Survival.*

The Patrimony of Africa would include our African Heritage, the fact that our descendants were slaves from Africa. This African Heritage manifests itself physically, culturally and institutionally. Further it has been said to manifest itself through ideas.

The Patrimony of Domination and Dependency focuses on domination from slavery until now. We can look at this in a number of different ways. Moving on from slavery, we take a historical stand. We were share-croppers, then we moved to the north and became the northern workers. Now we are still part of the unskilled labor forces of an industrial and technological society.

Next, there is dominance politically. We came all the way from a people who have been more or less disenfranchised. This was because we have not had political power or economic power.

Powerlessness can best be viewed as being characteristic of African-American people. This characteristic has many different expressions. Some people have been able to get into the system and use it, while others remain poor. The latter are the outcast and the underclass who make up the numbers living below the poverty line. So these are all characteristic of the African-American experience coming out of this legacy of slavery, and this legacy of oppression.

The third component of the African-American experience is the *Patrimony of Survival.* In defiance of the African trade heritage and this dominance/dependence relationship, African-American people have managed to survive. Their strength and resilience generates from their confidence in institutions such as: the extended family, the church, the lodges and the fraternities and sororities, all of which are prevalent in the African-American community.

Using these three components as a backdrop, the content and themes of the works of African-American women authors who write for adolescents will be examined. These writers have focused on the human experience, but more specifically, the experience that is unique to African-American people. Not included in this discussion will be works of fantasy, science fiction, biographies, autobiographies or folktales, rather the emphasis will be on contemporary realistic fiction and historical fiction. Theme one, the search for human freedom and dignity, is a category that could be sub-divided. The first sub-category would be characterized by contemporary stories in which the protagonist is faced with problems that threaten his/her self-worth and independence. This theme is carried out in the stories by Rosa Guy: *Ruby, Edith Jackson, The Disappearance* and *New Guys Around the Block;* Kristen Hunter's *The Soul Brothers and Sister Lou* and *Lou in the Limelight;* Dindga McCannon's *Wilhemina Jones, Future Star* and Ellease Southerland's *Let the Lion Eat Straw.*

The authors of the books in this first sub-category illustrate this theme through sound character development. *Ruby* and *Edith Jackson*, the adolescent protagonists in their respective novels, are plagued with the problems common to their age and stage of progression. These problems run the gamut from loneliness to peer acceptance. Ruby searches for self-worth and independence when she seeks love, comfort and companionship from a female peer. The author tells the story of an adolescent in transition and her struggle to become a woman in a family where over-protectiveness threatens to let this exist. Edith Jackson's fight for independence is skillfully chronicled against the backdrop of a society whose institutions have failed to work for the powerless. This is the story of an adolescent who vows to remove herself and three sisters from a foster home once she turns eighteen. In the novels, *The Disappearance* and *New Guys Around the Block*, Rosa Guy's protagonist escapes becoming another inner-city statistic. How easy it would have been for Imamu Jones to be devoured by the inevitability of the mean streets. Alternately, it was not to be for someone invested time in him. This allowed for a personable, intelligent young man to assume responsibility for his own action.

The Soul Brothers and *Sister Lou*, with its sequel *Lou in the Limelight*, shows how a group of inner-city adolescents, led by Louretta (Lou), accomplish their goal of becoming professional musicians. Their self-sufficiency is put to the test when they come face-to-face with the stark reality of "the real world of entertainment."

Dindga McCannon also permits her protagonist, Willi, in *Wilhemina Jones, Future Star*, to fulfill her dreams. Willi's fantasies include becoming a great painter and spending many years of happiness with her beloved boyfriend, Skeeter. The former has potential, while the latter suffers from all the characteristics of the typical adolescent love-romance formula.

Finally in this sub-category is *Let the Lion Eat Straw*. This is a story of Aloeba Williams who finds her world turned upside down when she must leave her rural surroundings after the death of her grandmother, who is her guardian. She moves to Brooklyn with her mother who resents having to take on this responsibility. The problems of adjusting to this very different environment with a parent she hardly knows sets the stage for this compelling story. Southerland permits her protagonist to experience all of life's changes from birth to death. She is permitted to grow in a natural and believable way. In the end, everyone who the protagonist has touched is the better for it.

In the second sub-category are stories that take their framework from periods in history that placed stringent demands on the book character as he/she struggles to maintain human freedom and dignity. Mildred Pitts Walter used the period of school desegregation as her settings in the *Girl on the Outside* and *Because We Are*. Virginia Hamilton sets *The House of Dies Drear* in contemporary times, but allows the character to momentarily return to his ancestral roots by having the family occupy a strange old mansion that was once a station on "the underground railroad." In *Roll of Thunder Hear My Cry* and *Let the Circle Be Unbroken*, Mildred Taylor allows her characters to live through the years of the "Great Depression" in rural Mississippi. The setting serves only to portray Cassie Logan, the protagonist, in a historical period in the Deep South when strained black-white relationships were precipitated by the ailing economy. Cassie is the product of a close-knit loving family that bands together to beat the odds.

Theme two, thinking and reacting independently, is a category of stories with unambiguous protagonists who are straight forward in their actions. This is the theme for the two stories by Sharon Bell Mathis: *Teacup Full of Roses* and *Listen for the Fig Tree*. *Rainbow Jordan* by Alice Childress and Hamilton's *M. C. Higgins, the Great* are stories that also depict self-sustaining characters who tackle problems unallied rather than waiting on others to initiate the action.

Surviving physically and mentally is the third theme. This is a relatively large category of stories with believable plots and characters who through their physical and emotional maturity, directly confront their environment. Generally, the authors use the inner-city as the setting for these stories. The protagonist faces such problems as the lack of security of a strong supportive family, the threat of gang violence and drugs and the problems that are inherent with extreme poverty. The Mathis and Hunter stories that were cited in theme one also find themselves in the category. To this list may be added: *Hero Ain't Nothing but a Sandwich* (Childress), *Sister* (Greenfield), and a very strong inner-city story by Virginia Hamilton, *The Planet of Junior Brown.*

The final theme is one that deals with relating to parents and peers. Age-mates and parent-child relationships are universal themes; however, these authors handle the issue in a manner that is unique to the African-American experience. Consider in this category titles such as *Growin'* (Nikki Grimes), *A Little Love* (Hamilton), *His Own Where* (Jordan), *The Friends* (Guy), *Sister* (Greenfield) and the afore-mentioned two titles by Mathis as exemplary. Likewise, the trilogy of Ludell: *Ludell, Ludell* and *Willie* and *Ludell's New York Times* by Brenda Wilkenson fit comfortably in this category. Rounding out this group are two titles by Joyce Carol Thomas: *Marked by Fire* and *Bright Shadow* that portray a very intriguing side of the African-American experience. The stories cited in this thematic discussion are relevant in that the writers are reflecting on the experiences that are unique to African-American people and are commenting from an African-American perspective.

In summary, it is interesting to note that with the exception of the few titles with late 1970's and early 1980's publication dates, it is apparent that these women are not getting published. The question then becomes, why is it that a generally accepted concept of the sixties: reflecting the experiences of all Americans in the literary offer-ings for children and adolescents, has now become forgotten or ignored?

One has only to look at recent publishers' catalogs or note book selection sources to see that there are fewer books being published for and about African-American children now than a decade or more ago. The number of African-American writers being published appeared to decrease when African-American political activity decreased. Additionally, as the Great Society government funds used to purchase minority materials were phased out, publishers simulta-neously began to phase out minority books. The practice of pre-publication censorship also adds to the decline. This occurs when manuscripts are selected for publication based not necessarily on the truth of their messages, but on how much they conform to the phi-losophy of the publishing firms. Many of the publishing houses are all a part of large corporate structures that make up the economic and political establishment of this country and thereby the profit-mak-ing element outweighs literary excellence.

As parents and educators, we have a responsibility to our children, both Black and White, to see that they are provided with quality literature that reflects all aspects of the human experience or minority experience in an atmosphere which is accurate and forthright. The African-American experience spans the world of women. This is evidenced in the writings of these women. Blacks and Whites have each in their own way made contributions to the African-American Experience in the past, in the present and will continue to do so in the future.

Reference
Thompson, Judith and Gloria Woodward, "Black Perspective Books for Children," *Wilson Library Bulletin*, 44:416-24, December, 1969.

Basic Themes in Realistic and Historical African-American Literature for Adolescents

I. Searching for human freedom and dignity
   a. Guy   e. Walter
   b. Hunter f. Hamilton
   c. McCannon   g. Taylor
   d. Southerland
II. Thinking and Reacting Independently
   a. Mathis
   b. Childress
   c. Hamilton
III. Surviving Physically and Mentally
   a. Mathis
   b. Guy
   c. Hunter
   d. Childress
   e. Greenfield
   f. Hamilton
IV. Relating to Parents and Peers
   a. Grimes
   b. Hamilton
   c. Jordan
   d. Guy
   e. Mathis
   f. Greenfield

g. Wilkenson
h. Thomas

Selected Bibliography of African-American Writers of Adolescent Literature

Childress, Alice. *A Hero Ain't Nothing But a Sandwich.* Coward, 1973.
Drug abuse and social conditions are the major focus of this story as Benjie Johnson, thirteen, is portrayed as a teenage heroin addict. The story is told by the use of dramatic monologues of several characters.

___ . *Rainbow Jordan.* Coward, 1981.
Fourteen-year old Rainbow has a particular concern, a delinquent mother. She is also beset by other, typical adolescent concerns. These include how to hold a boy without becoming his lover, and identifying and accepting the faults of a friend.

Greenfield, Eloise. *Sister.* Thomas Crowell, 1974.
This novel embraces many aspects of the human experience life, death, love, laughter and sadness. All of these are carefully documented by thirteen-year old Doretha (or 'Sister" as she is known to the family) in the book she calls her "Doretha Book" as she observes her older sister withdraw from the family following the death of the father.

Grimes, Nikki. *Growin'.* Illus. by Charles Lilly. Dial, 1977.
The relationship between Pump (Yolanda) and her mother is the binding factor in this story. Basically it is an episodic account of childhood, friendship and growing sensitivity and understanding that blossoms in preadolescents.

Guy, Rosa. *The Friends.* Holt, Rinehart and Winston, 1973.
Fourteen year-old Phyllisia Cathy has just moved to Harlem from the West Indies. Her adjustment to school is slow, coupled with the problems of coping with her strict father. She is befriended at school by Edith Jackson, a very sloven and unkept girl. At first Phyl refuses Edith's friendship, but eventually she comes to rely on it. Family problems are highlighted in this story.

____. *Ruby.* Viking, 1976.
This sequel to *The Friends,* tells of the older sister, eighteen-year-old Ruby and her transition from a girl to a woman. It tells a story of loneliness with all of its manifestations.

____. *Edith Jackson.* Viking, 1978.
This is the third in the trilogy of the West Indian family. Edith Jackson, Phyl's friend, tries to keep her family together after the death of their parents.

_____. *The Disappearance*. Delacorte, 1979.
Imamu Jones comes to live with the Aimsleys after the death of his father and the chronic alcoholism of his mother. This is an account of a streetwise Harlem-born youth who is wrongfully accused of murder.

_____. *New Guys Around the Block*. Delacort, 1983.
In the sequel to *The Disappearance*, Imamu has returned to his Harlem apartment. The tries to get a job, and plans to paint the apartment before his mother is released from the hospital where she's being treated for alcoholism. Still under suspicion by the police, Imamu asks his new friend Olivette to help him play detective.

Hamilton, Virginia. *M. C. Higgins. the Great*. MacMillan Co., 1974.
An Ohio hill boy tries to come to a decision about the future of his family and their home. Their safety has been threatened by a spoil heap remaining from strip mining.

_____. *The House of Dies Drear*. MacMillan, 1968.
Thomas Small's father has a college teaching position in a town in Ohio and has rented an old house that once served as an Underground Railroad Station. Set in contemporary times, this is a suspenseful story of the Small family and their experiences in Dies Drear's old house. Considerable information about slavery and the Underground Railroad is revealed.

_____. *The Planet of Junior Brown*. MacMillan, 1971.
This is a very intriguing story about inner-city life and three outcast teenagers who learn to survive by their wits. It is a story of Buddy Clark, a product of the streets, and the brotherhood he shares with other street children.

_____. *Zeely*. MacMillan, 1967.
This is the story of how Geeder is brought face-to-face with her African heritage.

Hamilton, Virginia. *A Little Love*. Philomel, 1984.
Sheema, the strong, touching character in this teenage love story, longs for the father who walked out when she was born and her mother died. The story focuses on her relationship with her grandparents who reared her and her steadfast love for Forrest, her teenage boyfriend.

Hunter, Kristen. *Guests in the Promised Land*. Scribner's, 1973.
A collection of eleven short stories that tell of the experiences of Black teenagers and the way they cope with their environment. The stories run the gamut from domineering mothers to rival street gangs.

_____. *The Soul Brothers and Sister Lou*. Scribner's, 1968.
Louretta Hawkins is torn between militancy and moderation in this

story of Black life in the urban ghetto and the impact it has on the youth. Pride in heritage, gang behavior, family life and the church are highlighted in this story.

____. *Lou in the Limelight*. Scribner's, 1981.

A sequel to *The Soul Brothers and Sister Lou*. The gang leaves home to make their way in the world of popular music. Instant success brings on problems as Lou tackles prevailing problems in a forthright and independent manner.

Jordan, June. *His Own Where*. Thomas Y. Crowell, 1971.

This is a poetically written love story of Buddy and Angela, friends and lovers. They turn their backs on society and begin to live their lives in an abandoned house in the cemetery as a means of escaping abusive and neglectful parents.

Mathis, Sharon Bell. *Teacup Full of Rose*. Viking Press, 1972.

There are elements of survival within this family living in an urban setting. Joe, Paul and Davey, three brothers, demonstrate their individual personalities which greatly impact on the family group. The story shows a family with needs and conflicts.

____. *Listen for the Fig Tree*. Viking Press, 1974.

Marvina (Muffin) Johnson, who is blind, lives alone with her alcoholic mother. This is a unique view of family and community support system.

McCannon, Dindga. *Wilhemina Jones, Future Star*. Delacorte, 1980.

Willi wants to be an artist in the worst kind of way but her mother is against it insisting that there is no future in art as a profession. This does not deter Willi anymore than her desire to love and be loved by Skeeter. Set in Harlem, this is a love story, and social protest statement combined. Skeeter is in boot camp and is soon shipped out to Vietnam. The story revolves around Willi's artistic aspiration and her desire to marry Skeeter and be on her own. She is dubbed "Future Star' when she wins an award at an art show.

Southerland, Ellease. *Let the Lion Eat Straw*. Scribner's 1979.

Abeba Williams grew up in the rural south but was reared in a Northern ghetto. This story speaks of her grandmother in the South and her mother in the North and the differences between the two. More importantly, it speaks of courage and honesty in the face of odds.

Taylor, Mildred. *Roll of Thunder Hear My Cry*. Dial, 1976

The setting for this story is the 1930's in rural Mississippi. It tells the story of the Logan family and their struggle to keep their land. Their struggles for human dignity and freedom are put to the test by the bigotry and racism that encompasses them.

____. *Let the Circle Be Unbroken*. Dial, 1981.

In this sequel to *Roll of Thunder, Hear My Cry,* the Logan family's story continues. It gives a picture of depression years in rural Mississippi and an indictment of Black-White relations in the deep south. Cassie, the only girl in the family, is a strong character whose strength is revealed throughout the book.

Thomas, Joyce Carol. *Marked by Fire.* Avon, 1982.

A fascinating story of life in Ponca City, Oklahoma, where (Abby) Abyssinia Jackson was born in a cotton field. The story tells of the healer, Mother Barker, and the secrets of folk medicine.

___ . *Bright Shadow.* Avon/Flare, 1983.

Abby, now twenty-years old, falls deeply in love with Carl Lee. Her father forbids her to see him and Abby is defiant. The break in the story comes when tragedy strikes and Carl Lee is able to show his gentleness and support to the family. This is an appealing love story with strong characters.

Walker, Mildred Pitts. *The Girl on the Outside.* Lothrop, Lee and Shepard, 1982.

The story depicts the events in Little Rock leading to desegregation of schools. The history that it relates makes this a memorable story. The book describes a strong relationship between Eva, the protagonist, her father and her boyfriend. The reader witnesses some of the arguments against desegregation by Black characters as well as the struggle of conscience that went on as some whites tried to convince others that change was needed in this country.

___ . *Because We Are.* Lothrop, Lee and Shepard, 1983.

This story chronicles a turbulent year when Emma, a middle-class Black high school senior learns how to channel her individual unwillingness to accept injustice into an ability to organize against it. The book shows character development as Emma comes to term with her own identity within the Black

Wilkinson, Brenda. *Ludell.* Harper and Row, 1975.

Ludell Wilson lives with her grandmother in a rural Georgia town while her mother is a live-in maid in New York. Next door lives Ludell's best friend, Ruthie Mae Johnson, whose brother Willie is Ludell's secret boyfriend; the two families are very close. Ludell experiences hardship and pleasure while growing up in the South of the 1950's.

___ . *Ludell and Willie.* Harper and Row, 1977.

In his sequel to *Ludell,* we find the protagonist now in high school and still living with her grandmother. Her love for Willie remains strong. Ludell's grandmother becomes ill and after she dies, Ludell reluctantly moves to New York to live with her mother.

___ . *Ludell's New York Time.* Harper and Row, 1980.

This is the trilogy to the books *Ludell,* and *Ludell and Willie.* Ludell has left her rural Georgia town after her grandmother's death to join her mother, Dessa, in Harlem. Not only does Ludell reluctantly leave the south, but she regrets having to leave her beloved Willie. Once in New York she works at a number of dead-end jobs, tries to adjust to the city life, but finds that her only desire is to marry Willie. Willie is drafted and Ludell vows, after quitting her job, to be with him as long as she can. Motherhood (Dessa) and its status are one of the themes in this compelling story.

The Family Chronicles of Mildred D. Taylor and Mary E. Mebane

Donnarae MacCann, Ph. D.
University of Iowa, Iowa City, Iowa

Mildred D. Taylor's novels and Mary E. Mebane's autobiography present separate strategies for uncovering social history. Being artists, the distinctness of their approach is inevitable. The socio-political subject matter is not inevitable, but it is also not surprising. Social injustice tends to be thematically prominent in African-American novels and autobiographies since conflicts stemming from discrimination affect even minor details of everyday life. As Taylor's principal character, Cassie Logan, notes in *The Road to Memphis* (1990), to merely exist in Mississippi in the 1930s-1940s was like being in a war.

Given the seriousness of the struggle, Taylor and Mebane reveal survival tactics in their stories, as well as underlying causes of the conflict. They illumine problems of subsistence and the importance of a close-kint community. Personal, social, economic, and political aspects of Black experience are skillfully interwoven. By showing the give-and-take between neighbors and family members, both authors imbue their narratives with a degree of reassurance a quality emphasized in traditional children's literature. Their works are true to that child-centered art form and true to a devastating period in American history:

the racist South from approximately 1930 to 1950.

That epoch is faithfully projected by Taylor and Mebane, but there is a double time frame that we need to keep in mind: the era described in the books and the historical moment that influenced both authors and audiences. In the children's book field in particular, a book will not go far within educational circles unless social and political institutions prove receptive. Children are part of a planned system an enculturation process that is controlled by the mainstream and serves mainstream interests. Children's books can be born only into *that world of social institutions that is willing to receive them.*

Taylor and Mebane were products of the 1960s, that moment in time that produced Martin Luther King, Jr.'s *Why We Can't Wait* (1964) and other history-making discourses of the Civil Rights Movement. Worldwide television coverage of that Movement (as it was evolving in Greensboro, Birmingham, etc.) created a small opening in mainstream consciousness and institutions. Entitlement programs for schools included money for multicultural books, and Mebane and Taylor stepped into that all-too-brief opening in "the system."

Both authors developed ways to highlight a vital principle in the Civil Rights Movement, namely, the connection between bigotry and economic exploitation. In *Why We Can't Wait*, King comments upon the visibility of this connection in the African-American community and the failure of some whites to recognize it:

> Many white Americans of good will have never connected bigotry with economic exploitation. They have deplored prejudice, but tolerated or ignored economic injustice. But the Negro knows that these two evils have a malignant kinship...
> The lowest-paid employment and the most tentative jobs were reserved for him [sic]. If he sought to change his position, he was walled in by the tall barrier of discrimination... Equality meant dignity and dignity demanded a job that was secure and a pay check that lasted throughout the week. (12)

Narratives by Taylor and Mebane prove that dynamic relationship between economics and race hatred, and upon that foundation, they are then able to offer a view of other social institutions: courts, schools, health and law enforcement agencies. In Taylor's major novels, *Song of the Trees* (1975), *Roll of Thunder, Hear My Cry* (1976), *Let the Circle Be Unbroken* (1981), *The Road to Memphis* (1990), the Logan family has a degree of economic security. Their four hundred acre farm is only partly mortgaged. In *Mary* (1981), Mebane describes a more fragile framework for subsistence. Economic survival is so tenuous that the resulting strain fractures family relationships. Such tension is explained by King as one of the underlying reasons "why we can't wait." He addresses the emotional dimensions of poverty and *shows how children are among the victims.* (153). In Mebane's *Mary*, family discord characterizes much of the protagonist's daily life. In Taylor's *Logan* series, we see this tragedy primarily in the lives of secondary characters.

The "Logans": Solidarity, Activism, Pastoral Values

Mildred D. Taylor came to the children's book field after training as a journalist. She wanted to present a literary "survival kit" based upon family history, as well as a literary entertainment for young readers. Upon winning the Newbery prize for *Roll of Thunder, Hear My Cry*, she explained that she was dissatisfied with the treatment of African-Americans in children's boooks. She noted that white writers had "failed to understand the principles upon which Black parents brought up their children and taught them survival." (*Newbery Award Acceptance*, 405). She clearly understood the subtle social aspects of childhood education the links between social responsibility, parenting, and the role of the creative artist. According to anthropologist James Spradley, child-rearing practices and community problem-solving are implicitly related. He writes: "The richest settings for discovering the rules of society are those where novices of one sort or another are being instructed in appropriate behavior." (21) The epic dimensions of the African-American experience and the child's role in that communal experience are underscored in Taylor's "*Logan*" stories. The interlocking life struggles of children and adults have rarely been presented more effectively. At the same time, life's affirmative side is vividly projected in family solidarity, social activism, and love of the land.

The short novel, *Song of the Trees*, was entered in the writers' contest sponsored by the Council on Interracial Books for Childrent, and won first place in the African-American division. Eight-year-old Cassie Logan narrates in a childlike, descriptive style:

I opened the window and looked outside. The earth

> was draped in a cloak of gray mist as the sun chased the nigh away. The cotton stalks, which in another hour would glisten greenly toward the sun, were gray. The ripening corn, wrapped in jackets of emerald and gold, was gray. Even the rich brown Mississippi earth and was gray.
>
> Only the trees of the forest were not gray. They stood dark, almost black, across the dusty road, still holding the night. A soft breeze stirred, and their voices whispered down to me in a song of morning greeting. (2)

Taylor places this unthreatening description of nature in sharp contrast to accounts of injustice and deprivation. The Logans struggle against poverty, an absent father, and the schemes of a white neighbor who decimates one of their groves. "Those trees that remained standing," says Cassie, "were like defeated warriors mourning their fallen dead." (35) As this family chronicle spreads over four separate novels, we see African-Americans compared with those "fallen dead," killed or disabled by night-riding terrorists, unfair court rulings, economic frauds, second-class schools, union-bursting, and numerous forms of intimidation.

All this politically important material is woven unobtrusively into the characters' lives. Big Ma, the Logan grandmother, faces the illegal ravaging of her whole forest, after agreeing to sell only a small portion. When the Logan children encounter the lumber-jacks, their reactions are plausible since we already know something of each character. Little Man is "a very small six-year-old and a most finicky dresser." To get him to breakfast takes persistence: "Call Little Man agin," says Mam. "Tell him he's not dressing to meet President Roosevelt this morning." (6) When a workman knocks him down and smudges his pants, the child strips, folds his clothes neatly, and only then takes after his tormentor with a stick. Christopher John is the sensitive, passive seven-year-old. He is reluctant to go along with his adventurous siblings, but even more terrified to be left behind. The eldest, Stacey, is torn between his desire for manhood status and his protected eleven-year-old status. He is thrust abruptly into maturity when sent to fetch his father in a neighboring state. Cassie is strong-willed, plain-spoken, and full of energy. These qualities make her an excellent narrator. That is, her characterization is convincing even when she turns up in unexpected places to serve as the eyes and ears of the reader.

Mr. Logan is the hard-working dad who "moonlights" on a Louisiana railroad job. He is in conflict with his neighbor, an ante-bellum type who covets the Logan woodlot and makes veiled threats:

> "I suggest you encourage Aunt Caroline [Big Ma] to sell them trees, Mary. You know, David [Mr. Logan] might not always be able to work so good. He could possibly have...an accident." (25)

When Papa and Mr. Andersen face off for the showdown, Papa voices a precept that is central to the whole Logan series:

> "One thing you can't seem to understand, Andersen," Papa said, "is that a black man's always gotta be ready to die. And it don't make me any dif-ference if I die today or tomorrow. Just as long as I die right." (49)

As Taylor's mouthpiece, Cassie becomes more important in the nov-els that follow. In *Roll of Thunder, Hear My Cry*, she is at the heart of a humiliating racial incident herself, but plays an even more impor-tant role in the author's literary method. Taylor gives Cassie a dou-ble perspective on the life that surrounds her. On the one hand, her diction and interpretation of events express a sophistication beyond her years. For example, she speaks of "reproval etching [Stacey's] face" when he cries, and friends who "sauntered over in feigned non-chalance." She is formal and analytical in describing the hired hand:

> On the front porch Mr. Morrison sat singing soft and low into the long night, chanting to the approaching thunder. He had been there since the house had darkened after church, watching and waiting as he had done every night since Pap had been injured. No one had ever explained why he watched and waited, but I knew. (185)

On the other hand, Cassie often uses a natural child voice, as when she warns her borther: "Mama's gonna wear you out." (1-2)

In short, Cassie comes across as both a naive and a mature nar-rator. The reader feels the presence of an astute, dispassionate reporter, and a childlike reporter simultaneoulsy. This device is not obtrusive because Taylor keeps the authorial voice subdued while the child-voice is a lively, oral voice and expresses the child-nature that Taylor knows so well.

Taylor's children are psychologically convincing without being overexplained. Little Man's finicky ways cause a classroom ruckus when he is repelled by second hand textbooks, throw-aways from the all-white school. In a scene in a country store, we see the young child's typical insistence upon codes of justice. Cassie understands the preferential treatment bestowed on adults, but expresses outrage when a white child, someone her own age, is given preferred treatment. She has yet to learn that whites in her region *always* constituted a privileged class. In an episode about the bus provided for white school children, the Logans express a child's typical sense of exaggerated guilt. (By making a hole in the road, they have taken revenge on the mean-spirited driver; but afterwards they feel agonizingly conspicuous and believe the "night riders" are after them).

Such glimpses of the child-mind are well-integrated with the political issues Taylor addesses. She does not lose the attention of the young audience, despite the sheer scope of historical coverage that makes this novel a groundbreaker. That coverage includes an account of the fraudulent crop lien system that kept sharecroppers forever in debt. It includes a view of various "legal" manuevers used by potential land-grabbers. It includes a picture of systematic, second-rate schooling, premeditated efforts to debase young adults, and the mob instinct behind lynchings. It includes a catalog of cruel harassments a major problem for Black children in their developing years.

Counteracting this oppression we see the survival strategies that mean aid for both adults and children: an extended family (an uncle, a grandmother, and a hired hand), a cooperating Black community, and a mainstream contact (a fair-minded lawyer). Equally important are a number of inner qualities such as self-respect, generosity, common sense, inner-direction all presented to the reader through plot, not platitude.

Only in children's literature, however, is survival as the Logans experienced it conceivable. Children's books make allowances for what amounts to guardian angels, characters who supply extraordinary assistance: e.g., Big Ma, a landowner due to the family's post-Civil War prosperity; Uncle Hammer, an economically successful Northerner; Mr. Morrison (the hired hand), "a human tree in height" a one-man defense force; Mr. Jamison, a lawyer with the Old

South roots that make him less vulnerable to attack than most non-conforming white Mississippians. Given such protectors, a happy ending can be logically contrived for the Logans. But to create a truly realistic novel about Mississippi in the Thirties would be to create a work outside the customary optimistic boundaries of children's literature.

To mitigate this artistic dilemma, Taylor invents an array of strong secondary characters. Either the Logan's neighbors or others in the region come closer to the reality, the no-win existence Martin Luther King analyzed in *Why We Can't Wait*. King insisted that human dignity was essential and that such dignity could not be sustained unless one had the wherewithal to feed one's family. Economic exploitation is the norm in Taylor's Mississippi and violence and intimidation are the means of sustaining it. The fatal burning of one sharecropper and the tarring and feathering of another these illustrate the systematic repression that Taylor uncovers for readers of *Roll of Thunder*.

In the next part of the series, secondary characters continue fighting a losing battle. Stacey's best friend in *Let the Circle Be Unbroken* is executed for a murder he does not commit. In *The Road to Memphis* another friend dies because the only available hospital has a "whites only" policy. Cassie's boyfriend, Moe Turner, barely manages to escape to the North after he defends Cassie from the white men who threaten and harass her.

In terms of technique, thematic material remains strong in both of these books, but *Let the Circle Be Unbroken* is the more compelling work. Perhaps this is because characterization is so basic to the art of the novel, and since the children have not aged significantly, their distinct personalities can be carried over in the mind of the reader from the earlier Logan books. Also Suzella, a fifteen-year-old mulatto cousin, enters the narrative and gives Taylor a chance to probe the subtleties of color consciousness and its many varied effects on people.

In *The Road to Memphis*, Cassie (now seventeen) is less plausible than she was at the age of eight or eleven. The novel seems obliged to meet the demands of that ambiguous sub-genre, the "teenage romance," and Taylor seems less ready to deal with the problems this entails.

But by the time we reach this fourth Logan story, place or setting is so important that it functions as character as the entity we watch with the most avid interest. Strawberry, Mississippi is like an ever-evolving personality, with new sides of its character shifting into light as new phases of Southern history take center stage. Cassie's function has been largely fulfilled in the earlier books.

Taylor is one in a stream of powerful writers rooted in the enlightened, albeit tumultuous, Sixties. Her special contribution was the successful linking of two traditional types of children's literature the family chronicle and the pastoral celebration with the conventions of the protest novel. Her skill is a sign of her uncompromising committment.

Race, Gender, and Class: The Triple Jeopardy in *Mary*

African-American scholars have frequently referred to the inter-relatedness of race, gender, and class, in critiquing the literary works of Black women. Critics have found the three-fold burden of racism, sexism, and classism expressed in all its complexity in Black feminist writings. That complexity, however, enters less often into books for the young. Mary E. Mebane's autobiographical *Mary* is an exception. It is an adult book fully accessible to the astute young adult a narrative showing the subtleties of race, gender, and class as embedded in the common routines of everyday life. Mebane begins with her childhood years and concludes with her graduation from North Carolina College in Durham. With exceptional eloquence, she lets us see those years as they were directly experienced, and the deeper meanings about historical time and place reach us despite Mebane's sparse use of editorial comments. Her analysis of her life becomes a panorama of a society plagued with racial, economic, and gender-based fallacies.

Mebane lets us see that mother-daughter misunderstandings are often traceable to hardships in a Black woman's life. With her child-eyes, Mary cannot be consciously aware of these social and economic strains. The wonder of Mebane's autobiography is the way the author maintains the child's perspective on events, but nonetheless reveals so much about the gender-based contraint(s) upon her mother, herself, and their many female acquaintances.

Similarly, Mary does not realize in any conscious sense that white racism weighs upon her father, that it creates psychological pressures as well as political and economic deprivations. Her father's efforts to remove his family as far as possible from the influence of racism, and his resistance to the bureaucratic Establishment in those small details of life where he could exercise some authority these aspects of her father's character shed a bright light upon the biased social environment of rural North Carolina.

A destructive classism invades Mary's life when she takes the small legacy provided by her Aunt Jo and enrolls in college. The elites on the campus love to flaunt their exalted status and display their scorn for "country" folk.

Mebane uses a straightforward, three-part structure that enables her to capture the inner and outer essences of childhood and its first lessons, teenage life and the grueling work of an assembly line, and young adulthood in a less than satisfying college community.

Part I covers the years 1933-1947. During this time and for years afterward, Mary perceives her mother as a cold, hardhearted person. Mebane tells of the night her mother sent her out "in the dark alone [to the outhouse] and in the pouring rain. I was five years old. Eden had ended for me." (37) That this experience took on extraordinary importance in her memory is not surprising:

> ...I was even more scared of my mother now that she
> was mad; so I went running out into the rain in my
> nightgown. While I was out there I don't remem-
> ber whether I was coming back or still going some-
> thing or someone came up behind me and pushed
> me down. I jumped up fast, running to get away
> from it. I had been hurt. (37)

Other details about this happening are blocked from memory, but the terror of that night was a watershed in the child's early life. And her mother, Nonnie, was the one who was blamed. Mary had run to her father and some carpenters who were sleeping in the barn [carpenters were there to build a new house], but her father simply advised: "Go back to your mother."

Nonnie is easy to place in that category of women that Zora Neale Hurston called the "mule of the world" persons compelled to demonstrate superhuman strength. Nonnie was a fulltime tobacco factory worker, a fulltime farm wife, and the parent of three children. She was giving support in the same sense that Toni Morrison shows support for children in her novel *Sula*. In that story, the fictional Eva is said to love her children by staying alive for them. Nonnie's loving was similarly practical rather than symbolic, but her daughter missed the outward signs the warm lap and words of approval.

This mother-daughter relationship is also undermined by Mary's high susceptibility to fantasies circulated in the white press. She is filled with images of affluent white families, a world placed at her very doorstep through her father's junk collecting business.

> Sometimes there would be magazines in the trash and I would save them to look at when I was by myself. I would sit quietly and look at the pictures. There were dresses and houses and mothers kissing children and men kissing women and beautiful things that I had never seen before. When I got to the end, I would start at the beginning again. Soon I learned not to turn the pages so fast; it would last longer if I looked at the same picture a long time. (23)

Besides the sense of emotional deprivation, apparently stimulated by these glamorous magazines, Mary endures an intellectual alienation from her mother. Her Aunt Jo, a member of the household for several years, unknowingly exacerbated the distance between mother and daughter by developing Mary's skills as a classical pianist. With the help of Mrs. Shearin, Mary's teacher, Aunt Jo introduces her niece to the delights of Chopin and the intellectual enrichment of *Etude* magazine. All this gives Mary cultural reference points that she cannot share. In her music she finds an independent and expressive voice, but she becomes a marginal character in her family and circle of companions. Not even the trials and triumphs of the Black concert singer, Marian Anderson, interests Mary's friends.

Mary develops as an artist, but like other African-American children she sees examples of race discrimination that frustrate a normally evolving self-esteem. For instance, she admires a handsome chinaware cup donated to her little brother, but then learns that the white owner had discarded it rather than "contaminate" herself by drinking from a cup used by a Black person. This is the kind of insult that caused Rufus, Mary's father, to move his family farther and farther into the hinterland.

Ruf is a perpetual target of discrimination and he is repeatedly hampered as a breadwinner. He sees his white childhood friend advance as an entrepreneur, while he is rejected by every factory in town. It is not surprising that the whole Mebane family watched eagerly for the upcoming boxing matches of the Black athlete, Joe Louis. "If Joe Louis, a black man, won," writes Mebane, "Daddy had won." It was a sad commentary on American life, she explains, when one's positive self-image depended upon the projected image of a single person. Yet when Louis won, Ruf looked the look that said, "'Joe Louis won. He is black like me; therefore, that means that I won, too. I am not nothing. I am something.'" (73)

In Part II, after Ruf's death in 1947, Mary moves into the dehumanizing environment of a Southern tobacco factory. Work on the assembly line is so backbreaking that even such an inveterate book-lover as Mary suffers from a numbing exhaustion and gives up reading. Eventually she tries another job providing child care for a white family but is left stranded without her pay. She has no contractural protection and no redress when the family she works for breaks up and leaves their employees wageless.

In the last section, Part III, we have a glimpse of Mary's life as a college student. Knowing that her niece has out-performed her peers academically, Aunt Jo continually reinforces the idea that Mary is clearly cut-out for college. But the priorities of students reflect an entrenched racism and classism. The first necessity for a female student is to possess a chic wardrobe; the second is to be on the "right" side of the color line. Mebane had all the "flaws" of the person she dubs "the black black woman."

> Facial features that were not typically black were felt to be beautiful: lips that were not full and a nose that was not broad. My mouth and nose were full... My hair, as was the case with most girls in the school, was not shoulder-length and was not naturally straight...
> But canceling out all "defects" for a girl was a "light skin." Light skin was really banana-colored, though often a girl with caramel-colored skin could make it over into the beautiful category if she had long or straight hair. I varied...from a fade-out black in winter to a reddish-chocolate after a summer in the sun.(77-78)

Later Mebane notes that "if nature had painted one more brush-stroke on me, I'd have had to kill myself."

Mebane's character sketches reveal the complex interaction of race, gender, and class, but the point is not made explicitly. Perhaps because she is not gearing her work for a young audience *per se*, she is able to use more understatement than Mildred Taylor. Mebane is taking a deep, introspective look at her region and era, whereas

Taylor is blending fact and fiction for young readers and uses a more conscious, programmatic approach (as she admits when she speaks of her plan to illumine African-American survival tactics). But since the era and setting are much the same, the two writers offer similar instances of discrimination. Mebane describes the same kind of humiliation that Taylor's Little Man faces when his teacher distributes secondhand books. She writes:

> I bent over the box to get a book, and grasped it the wrong way; it fell open to a page that had yellow tape on it. I was about to close the book when I saw the words PROPERTY OF BRAGGTOWN SCHOOL... We were paying rent for books that the white children at the brick school had used last year... All of them were secondhand. They felt dirty to me. I wondered about the girl who had had my book last year. She was smug and laughing at me. I had to use her old book. It wasn't right. (61).

She also describes the anger and fright stemming from Jim Crow laws. As Cassie Logan was forced to pay homage to a white child of the same age, so the Blacks on a North Carolina bus endured a similar code of "white supremacy." They were forced to yield up their seats if the Durham buses had no space but standing room. Mebane described a particular case and emphasizes the irony of wartime equality versus peacetime discrimination:

> The white man who had just gotten on the bus walked to the seat in no-man's-land and stood there... Two adult males, living in the most highly industrialized, most technologically advanced nation in the world, a nation that had devastated two other industrial giants in World War II and had flirted with taking on China in Korea. Both these men, either of whom could have fought for the United States in Germany or Korea, faced each other in mutual rage and hostility... (162-163)
> "Say there, buddy, how about moving back," the driver said..." "Say buddy, did you hear me?"

In addition to similarities in content, Mebane and Taylor share a double rhetorical style, a way of suggesting the aura of childhood while still allowing for a more analytical treament of a subject. For example, Mary's eight-year-old voice and perspective is noticeable when she begins a description of life in the third grade:

> Mrs. Richardson, the third-grade teacher, was a pretty lady. She had a gold chip between her teeth and she smiled a lot. She had light-brown skin and wore her hair pulled back in a bun. She liked to say, "Now boys and girls..." She liked me. (65)

At the other extreme, we sometimes see the author's mature consciousness, as when she employs complex sentences and puzzles over the plight of a misfit:

> You harbor the guilty knowledge that you do not belong. But even worse, you follow the group's belief that you do not belong because there is something intrinsically the matter with you; that all family groupings are just alike,... and since other people seem to be living harmoniously in a grouping of some kind, while you are in misery all the time, something or someone has decreed that you must be an outsider, that something being God or Fate or whatever governs human affairs; that you must be an outsider for an unspecified length of time to atone for some secret sin that you somehow, somewhere in the past, committed; that you must submit to harsh accusations, cruel judgments, uncomplainingly. (30-31)

To sum up, Mebane's technique contains a blend of simplicity and complexity, as a writer's style must if it is to bring to light the perspectives of both mature and immature characters. In an overall evaluation of Mary and tribute to Mebane as a stylist, Marion Meade praises this author's images of rural living, all skillfully "pieced together into an exquisite mosaic." And she adds: "Mebane is incapable of putting a word on paper that stays there; it leaps up and assaults the senses." (28-29)

With respect to content, nowhere is the race/gender/class dynamic shown in a clearer light than in a scene where Nonnie chides her daughter and Mary explains the source of the trouble:

> I was guilty. Washing and ironing, the measure of
> achievement for community girls, interested me not
> at all. For unspoken was the knowledge that these
> black girls were really being trained to work as
> domestics, not to keep house for themselves. But
> they and their mothers played a game that they were
> learning to be good housekeepers... (113)

To be a Black woman was to be exploited and face disadvantaged on
three fronts. Mebane's analytical mind and eye for detail make that
conclusion unmistakeable.

Conclusion

Both Taylor and Mebane document the ways in which some measure of success can occur even under the most difficult and even
tragic circumstances. But alongside the progressive life experiences
of the few, they show us the plight of the many. Their works challenge the "democracy" of tokenism a political system that treats
democracy as nothing more than a promise. Martin Luther King, Jr.
made this point in 1964 and defined tokenisms as a policy that allows
a few to succeed, while the mainstream assumes that those few can
serve to represent the many. (19-20) Countering that false assumption, he puts to us the question: "How can we make freedom real
and substantial?" (148) That question lies implicitly within *Mary*
and the series about the Logans; and Mebane and Taylor suggest an
answer by showing what happens when some people have opportunities and some do not. We will still need that insight in the upcoming century.

Notes

1. Mildred D. Taylor was born in Jackson, Mississippi in 1943. Three
   weeks later her father was involved in a racial incident and decided
   to promptly move his family to the North. Taylor graduated from
   the University of Toledo, spent two years in Ethiopia with the Peace
   Corps, and then earned her Master of Arts degree in the University
   of Colorado's School of Journalism. Mary E. Mebane grew up on
   the outskirts of Durham, North Carolina, earned a B.A. from North
   Carolina College, and M.A. and Ph.D. from the University of North
   Carolina at Chapel Hill. She teaches at the University of Wisconsin
   in Milwaukee.
2. Two more short novels *The Friendship* (1987) and *Mississippi Bridge*
   (1990) include the Logan children, plus additiolnal adult charac-

ters who are the main focus of the narratives. Both stories expose facets of prejudice and social injustice.

3. The Council of Interracial Books for Children (CIBC) began an annual writers' competition for African-Americans shortly after it was founded in 1966. CIBC later extended the contest to include Native American, Hispanic, and Asian writers whose manuscripts were, as yet, unpublished. The contest was terminated in the early Eighties due to a shortage of funds. CIBC is a non-profit organization that encourages anti-racist and anti-sexist children's literature.

4. The crop lien system was a credit system in which local merchants furnished supplies to planters and sharecroppers in exchange for a lien on the growing crops. Interest rates often exceeded 50%, and merchants' bookkeeping procedures were sometimes dishonest; in short, the system faciliated constant indebtedness and constant dependency of Black sharecroppers on the white business establishment.

5. See, for example, Bell Hooks' *Feminist Theory from Margin to Center* (South End Press, 1984).

6. The sequel to *Mary, Wayfarer* (1983) is another remarkable book, but is, in my view, for adult readers.

Works Cited

King, Jr., Martin Luther. *Why We Can't Wait*. New York: Harper and Row, 1964.

Meade, Marion. Rev. of *Mary*, by Mary E. Mebane. *Ms. Magazine*, X:1 (July 1981) 28-29.

Mebane, Mary E. *Mary*, New York: Fawcett Juniper ed., 1982; Hardcover Ed.: Vicking, 1981.

Spradley, James. *Culture and Cognition*. San Francisco: Chandler, 1972.

Taylor, Mildred D. *Let the Circle Be Unbroken*. New York: Dial Press, 1981.

_____. Newbery Award Acceptance. Horn Book Magazine, (August 1977) 401-409.

_____. The Road to Memphis. New York: Dial Press, 1990.

_____. Roll of Thunder, Hear My Cry. New York: Bantam Books, 1978; Hardcover Ed.: Dial Press, 1976.

_____. Song of the Trees. New York: Bantam Skylark Books, 1978; Hardcover Ed.: Dial Press, 1975.

Master of Nonfiction: James Haskins

Joan Nist, Ph.D.
Auburn University, Alabama

When the Newbery Medal for outstanding U.S. children's books was instituted in the early 1920's, the first recipient was a work of nonfiction: Hendrik Van Loon's *The Story of Mankind* (1921). Thereafter, however, the award winners through the years were overwhelmingly from the genre of fiction/fantasy. Recently there has been a trend back toward recognition for well-written nonfiction. The Newbery itself was awarded in 1988 to Russell Freedman for *Lincoln: A Photobiography* (1987), and a new award, the Orbis Pictus, begun by the National Council of Teachers of English to honor nonfiction, has been received by Jean Fritz (1990) and Freedman (1991).

Other writers of informational books have achieved stature comparable to the Newbery Medal/Honor authors, for instance Milton Meltzer, Millicent Selsam, and Laurence Pringle. Among outstanding nonfiction writers is James Haskins, author or co-author of over a hundred books, many depicting aspects of African-American culture and others devoted to the accomplishments of outstanding Americans of African descent.

Haskins himself is an African-American, so he writes from the first-hand perspective of a member of the culture. He does not, however, represent a narrow view. His interests and abilities go beyond ethnicity and nationality. An educator, he has studied and writen about such varied topics as language, music, psychology/sociology, and sports.

Haskins was born in Alabama in 1941. He received a B.A. in psychology from Georgetown University in 1960, and a B.S. in history from Alabama State University two years later. His master's degree, in social psychology, was earned at the University of New Mexico in 1963, and he subsequently did further graduate study in New York. The quality of his work led to his election into Phi Beta Kappa, the prestigious scholastic honor society. He has continued his academic connections, for since 1977 he has been a professor in the Department of English at the University of Florida.

Before beginning his teaching career, he had positions with the New York Department of Welfare, the New York *Daily News,* and the stockbroker firm of Smith, Barney and Company. His experiences as a teacher led to writing, and *Diary of a Harlem Schoolteacher* was published in 1969 (Grove; reissued: Stein and Day, 1979). Since then, every year has seen publication of new books by Haskins.

Many of the titles in his extensive bibliography are biographies, often of the achievements of African-Americans, with an emphasis on their contributions to their professions and to overall culture. That he is not restricted by racial or patriotic limits is shown by two examples of his sport-hero biographies. The glamor figure of the major American sport, baseball, is the long-distance hitter, and appropriately, when Haskins wrote about the best, it turned out to be *Both Babe Ruth and Hank Aaron: The Home Run Kings* (Lothrop, Lee & Shepard, 1974), one white, one black, one from early years, the other more recent. And he recognized the most famous worldwide athlete of his time, whose sport ironically is not major in the U.S. the great soccer star *Pele: A Biography* (Doubleday, 1976) of Edson Arantes Do Nascimento of Brasil.

The most famous of Haskin's works is probably *The Cotton Club* (Random House, 1977; New American Library, 1984), on which the movie directed by Francis Ford Coppola was based. An example of Haskins' historical scholarship, the book is profusely illustrated with photographs. In contrast, some of his recent writing has been in picture-book form and reflects his continuing interest in language and desire to give young readers insights into other cultures. Using the numbers 1 through 10, he presents bits of information about the arts, history, and folkways of twelve differing groups: *Count Your Way Through Africa, ...Canada, ...China, ...Germany, ...India, ...Israel, ...Italy, ...Japan, ...Korea, ...Mexico, ...Russia, ...the Arab World*

(Carolrhoda, 1987-1990). For example, in *Count Your Way Through the Arab World:* "In Arabic, there are *eight* different ways to say cousin." In *Count Your Way Through China:* "All Chinese music is based on a musical scale of *five* tones."

Music has been one of the major themes for Haskins' work. His biographies of musical figures range from the legendary *Lena: A Personal and Professional Biography of Lena Horne* (with Kathleen Benson, Stein and Day, 1984), who is still singing after many decades, to *The Story of Stevie Wonder* (Lothrop, Lee & Shepard, 1976), who is not only an accomplished musician but also an example of the capability of the disabled. The latter shows yet another group of people about whom Haskins has written: *Who Are the Handicapped?* (Doubleday, 1978) and *The Quiet Revolution: The Struggle for the Rights of Disabled Americans* (with J. M. Stifle, Crowell, 1979).

Among Haskins' most significant work outside the biographical form are three comprehensive studies which use sociological as well as historical and biographical approaches: *Black Theater in America* (Crowell, 1982). *Black Music in America: A History Through Its People* (Crowell, 1987), and the recent *Black Dance in America: A History Through Its People* (Crowell, 1990). These books document interesting narrative black contributions to American culture in these three art forms. For instance, in the most recently published, Haskins chronicles the beginning of *Black Dance* as the exercise called "dancing the slaves" and states that "From 'jazz dancing' to 'break dancing,' modern dance is heavily influenced by African dance forms. At the same time, many of today's black dancers are stars in traditional white forms of dance, like ballet..." (p. 14)

The works of outstanding African-American imaginative authors like Virginia Hamilton, Mildred Taylor, and Walter Dean Myers are recognized as part of the canon of American children's/ youth literature. This brief introduction to James Haskins, one of the prolific and capable nonfiction writers in the field, can lead readers to an account of his work in his own words in *Something About the Author Autobiography Series* (Volume 4) and, most important, to some of his many books. A selected bibliography (in addition to works already cited) follows, showing the broad range of topics on which Haskins has written.

Selected Bibliography
About Michael Jackson, Enslow, 1985.

Always Movin' On: The Life of Langston Hughes. Watts, 1976.

Andrew Young, Man With A Mission. Lothrop, Lee Shepard, 1979.

Aretha: A Personal and Professional Biography. (With Kathleen Benson) Stein and Day, 1986.

The Autobiography of Rosa Parks. (With Rosa Parks) Dial, 1990.

Barbara Jordan. Dial, 1977.

Bill Cosby: America's Most Famous Father. Walker, 1988.

The Child Abuse Help Book. (With Pat Connolly) Addison-Wesley, 1982.

The Consumer Movement Watts, 1975.

Corazon Aquino: Leader of the Philippines. Enslow, 1987.

The Creoles of Color of New Orleans. Crowell, 1975.

Doctor J: A Biography of Julius Ervin. Doubleday, 1975.

Double Dutch. (With David A. Walker) Enslow, 1986.

Fighting Shirley Chisholm. Dial, 1975.

From Lew Alcindor to Kareem Abdul-Jabbar. Rev. ed. Lothrop, Lee & Shepard, 1978.

Gambling Who Really Wins? Watts, 1979.

The Guardina Angles. Enslow, 1983.

Hamp: An Autobiography. (With Lionel Hampton) Warner, 1989.

India Under Indira and Rajiv Gandhi. Enslow, 1989.

Jokes From Black Folks. Doubleday, 1973.

Leaders of the Middle East. Enslow, 1985.

The Long Struggle: The Story of American Labor. Westminster, 1976.

Mr. Bojangles: The Biography of Bill Robinson. (with N. R. Nitgang) Morrow, 1988.

The New Americans: Cuban Boat People. Enslow, 1982.

Outward Dreams: Black Inventors and Their Contributions. Walker, 1991.

Real Estate Careers. Watts, 1978.

Religions of the World. Rev. ed. Hippocrene, 1991.

Shirley Temple Black: Actress to Ambassador. Viking Kestrel, 1988.

Snow Sculpture and Ice Carving. Macmillan, 1974.

The Statue of Liberty, America's Proud Lady. Lerner, 1986.

Teen-age Alcoholism. Hawthorn, 1976.

Werewolves. Watts, 1981.

Your Rights, Past and Present: A Guide for Young People. Hawthorn, 1975.

The Coretta Scott King Award

Lee Bernd
Bookworms, Stone Mountain, Georgia

On July 2, 1991, more than 800 American Library Associations members and guests assembled in the Grand Ballroom of the Atlanta Hilton to pay tribute to this year's winners of the prestigious Coretta Scott King Award. The award recognizes African American authors and illustrators whose distinguished books for children and young adults promote an understanding and appreciation of the culture and contribution of all people to the realization of the American dream.

The Medal commemorates the life and work of Martin Luther King, Jr. At the same time it honors his widow, Coretta Scott King, for her courage and determination in working for peace and world brotherhood. The medal resulted from another dream, that of a noted African American children's librarian Glyndon Greer. She has said that as she thought about Martin Luther King's words, "I have a dream," she knew she'd been dreaming of an award to recognize and encourage African American authors of children's books. She worked tirelessly to make her personal dream come true. And by 1969 she had enough support to establish the Award at the annual ALA Conference in Atlantic City, New Jersey. The first award was given in 1970; in 1974 an award was added for an illustrator. Also in 1974, the award headquarters moved to Atlanta, where Atlanta artist Lev Mills designed the official award seal. The bronze seal on a book designates the winner while the silver seal means the book received honorable mention.

By 1982 the Coretta Scott King Award for authors and illustrators was declared an official ALA award. Each year, at the ALA annual convention, a ceremony recognizes the winning authors and illustrators. Fittingly, the subject of the first award was the man with the dream. The book was *Martin Luther King, Jr., Man of Peace*, by Lillie Patterson. A powerful biography which has set a standard not often achieved in either adult or children's books, it is as readable and dramatic today as it was when published more than twenty years ago. The author has also been honored for another biography of Dr. king; one of Coretta Scott King; and the story of Benjamin Banneker, the architect who designed Washington, D.C.

A recipient of two awards and six honorable mentions is Virginia Hamilton, considered one of children's literature's finest writers. Surely she is among the most decorated, having won the Newbery National Book Award, and Boston Globe Awards. Her 1986 winner is a stunning collection, *The People Could Fly: American Black Folktales*. Animal tales and stories of the real, extravagant, fanciful, and supernatural, and slave tales of freedom are narrated in breathtaking prose and stunningly illustrated by Caldecott artists, Leo and Diane Dillon.

Another esteemed writer, Mildred D. Taylor, has received three Coretta Scott King Awards. *Let The Circle Be Unbroken*, her 1982 winner, is a sequel to *Roll of Thunder, Hear My Cry*, a Newbery Medal winner. Taylor's 1988 winner, *The Friendship*, is, like the preceding books, based on her family's experiences in the South during the Depression. In 1980, 1985, 1989, Walter Dean Myers received the medal. The first two winners, *The Young Landlords* and *Motown and Didi*, are realistic pictures of older, street-wise, city children. At 17 Myers joined the army; he remembers himself as a kid from Harlem with a romantic picture of war. *Fallen Angels*, his 1989 winner, comes out of his own experiences in Vietnam, where he, like his fictional hero learned the truth about war.

But not all the books are serious. *Justin and the Best Biscuits in the World* by Mildred Pitts Walter is a delightful read-aloud. On a visit to Grandpa's ranch, ten-year-old Justin learns about the exodusters, former slaves who went West to become cattle ranchers and cowboys. He's proud to learn of his family's past and bursting to show that he can make the world's best biscuits.

Poset Eloise Greenfield received the 1990 medal for *Nathaniel Talking*, raps and rhymes of a nine-year-old. Most of them are joyous and spontaneous.

Through other winners, young readers learn of a number of African American heroes: Barbara Jordan, Mary McCleod Bethune, Andrew Young, Billie Holiday, and Lena Horne, whose lives can enrich and inspire. Winner of the 1978 award is Carole Byard, who, through a Ford Foundation grant, was able to visit Africa. Her life-long dream to visit her home had come true. This gifted author/artist has produced unforgettable portraits in text and illustration, in the award-winning book, *Africa Dream*. In 1980 she received the illustrator medal for her hauntingly beautiful pictures in *Cornrows*, a book which explains the symbolism of this old African custom. Ms. Byard is the only person who has received both the author and illustrator medals.

Another book of amazing portraits is *Something on My Mind*, with pictures by Tom Feelings. In fact, his art inspired prize-winning Nikki Grimes' poetic prose. Here are views of children experiencing the whole gamut of human emotions.

In *Beat the Story Drum, Pum, Pum*, Ashley Bryan offers new insight into the heart of Nigerian culture. In retelling five traditional tales, he uses repetition, rhyming phrases, and alliteration; the illustrations in brick red, mustard yellow, and black resemble wood cuts. The book equally pleases eye and ear. Two additional collections of folk tales and one of Christmas spirituals have also been named honor books. Illustrator Jerry Pinkney has received the illustrator medal three times. In *Mirandy and Brother Wind*, young Mirandy wants to capture Brother Wind for her partner in the junior cakewalk contest. This beautiful book provides a delightful introduction to a dance African slaves brought to America. *The Patchwork Quilt* is a touching story; in words and text one meets a loving, strong African American family, a vision seldom seen in children's books.

Joe Steptoe received the medal for *Mufaro's Beautiful Daughters*, which had already received a Caldecott silver medal and the Boston Globe-Horn Book Award for illustration. He aimed to create a book that included things that had been left out of his own education about the people who were his ancestors. Many feel it is the finest picture book of the past twenty years. In this masterpiece and his other works, Steptoe successfully challenges the status quo by creating for African American children, literature which reflects themselves and their lives. In so doing, he extends the world of children's books for everyone readers of all colors and all races.

Leo and Diane Dillon have received the Caldecott Medal twice.

This year they received the illustrator award for Leontyne Price's AIDA. Individually the artists have their own styles, but when they work together, as they have since 1957, they are as one artist. This elegantly designed and brilliantly executed book is one of their finest achievements.

Honored at the same meeting was author Mildred Taylor for *The Road to Memphis*, another volume in the continuing Logan family saga. In her acceptance speech, she said she wanted to tell her father's story so that young people would never forget the way it was and determine that it will never be that way again.

Through books like those discussed here, readers of every background can come to understand and appreciate African-American culture and contributions. When that is achieved, we may all come closer to realizing Martin Luther King's dream of the day when all God's children will join hands and sing.

The International Context of African-American Children's Literature

Dianne Johnson, Ph.D.
University of South Carolina

From January 1920 through December 1921, W.E.B. DuBois and Augustus Granville Dill published "a little magazine for children for all children, but especially for ours, 'the children of the sun'... It will be called, naturally, *The Brownies Book,* and as we have advertised, "It will be a thing of Joy and Beauty, dealing in Happiness, Laughter and Emulation." The description continues: "It will seek to teach Universal Love and Brotherhood for all little folk black and brown and yellow and white. Of course, pictures, puzzles, stories, letters from little ones, clubs, games, and oh everything!"

This description is interesting particularly because of its optimistic tone. The line advocating love and brotherhood only hints at the pan-African, international, socially progressive perspective that it does, in fact, demonstrate consistently; a perspective which entails controversy and whatever else is the opposity of joy, happiness, and laughter.

The statement is interesting, too, in an historical context, specifically in relationship to *Ebony Jr!* (Chicago: The Johnson Publishing Co., 1973-1985), the African-American children's magazine of the 1970s. My contention is that the demise of the latter magazine came about because of its own self-limitations in terms of its guidelines for contributing writers. These guidelines not only emphasize the value placed on positive representation of African-American people, but they ask writers, explicitly, not to submit materials which deal with death, violence, or religion.

But for the editors of *The Brownies' Book* (New York: DuBois and Dill, 1920-1921), in contrast, it was not only undesirable, but impossible to ignore such issues. They understood that acculturating, socializing, and educating African-American children as United States and world citizens meant discussing with them quite serious social and psychological dilemmas. During the years when the magazine was in publication, *St. Nicholas* (NY: Scribner, 1873-1945), the preeminent mainstream American children's magazine was publishing verses such as "Ten little nigger boys went out to dine. One choked his little self and then there were nine." DuBois's reaction to such representations (and lack of representations at all) was that "all of the Negro child's idealism, all his sense of the good, the great and the beautiful is associated with white people. He unconsciously gets the impression that the Negro has little chance to be great, heroic or beautiful." (1920, 2:63).

In response, *The Brownies' Book* regularly demonstrated to African-American youth the complex ways in which they and the members of their communities were, in deed, all of these things. Thus, when *St. Nicholas* shows children who are "proud to be the nieces and nephews of Uncle Sam," (Elinor Sinnette, 1965. "The Brownies' Book: A Pioneer Publication for Children." *Freedomways* 5:133-142) *The Brownies Book* pictures African-American Sunday school children marching in protest to the lynchings and brutalities of the South. The current events section of *St. Nicholas* reports in April 1920 that "Those restless people beyond the Rio Grande spent the month of April in their favorite pastime Civil War." (Sinnette, same as preceding). In contrast, *The Brownies' Book* offers a more detailed and complex report, stating that "There has been a revolution in Mexico. President Carranza has been expelled and General Obregon is at the head of most of the opposing forces. The trouble seems to have been that Carranza was not willing to have what his rivals considered a fair election" (Sinette, same as preceding piece).

The concern with world affairs and cultures worldwide is evident in every section of the magazine. Contributors submit games, songs, stories, and folklore from around the world. Letters were submitted from Caucasian readers, Filipino youngsters, and Cuban children, among others. It is clear in every section of the publication that what goes on in one's own personal life as well as in an individual society affects what happens in other individual lives and societies.

Consider the following, rather extended excerpt from the column entitled "The Judge." In it, the Judge responds to young Wilhelmina's reasoning about buying new clothes and her complaints of being treated like a child by her parents. The Judge replies:

> How do you know you like that hat? Is it suited to you? Does it really set off your figure and your smooth, brown skin? Or, and here I have a deep suspicion, do you choose it because Katie Brown has one like it and the Ladies of Avenue K, and but hold! Who are K.B. and the L. of A.K.? Are they persons of taste, or simply of power? Do you imitate them for love, or fear? Does the choice of this hat represent your freedom of thoughtful taste, or your slavery to what the flamboyant Kitty does or to what rich white folk wear?
> Mind you, I'm not answering these questions I'm just asking. We will assume that the hat is becoming and suits you and you want it. Now comes that awkward question of money. What is the question of Money? Simply this: Of the 1,000 ways of spending this dollar, which is best for me, for mother, for the family, for my people, for the world? If the "best" way of spending it for you makes mother starve, or the family lose the home, or colored folk be ridiculed, or the world look silly why, then, no such hat for you, and that, too, by your own dear Judgment (1920, 1:12-13).

I've quoted this passage at length for several reasons. First, it's a forceful example of the tone of the magazine. It's weighty, to say the least. What saves it from being almost demoralizing is that the reader realizes that she/he has choice and can exercise individual judgment. Secondly, the passage demonstrates my point concerning the international context in which *The Brownies' Book* is constructed. The emphasis of the passage is on the interconnectedness of the actions and decisions of the countless individuals who are, in fact, world citizens. In this particular passage, this interrelatedness is couched in terms of economic relationships.

What I wish to call attention to, however, are the class implications of the passage. Not only does it invoke the ideas of freedom of taste (or choice) and power (in relationship to other black people as well as to rich white people), but even mentions Wilhelmina's skin color. It is significant that these ideas are framed within what seems to be a larger, more significant context because, in fact, it becomes apparent when examining the whole of the magazine that notions such as economic status, "taste," and color are intimately related to the global experience of African-Americans.

Simply, put, at the same time that DuBois and other African-Americans are promoting a pan-African perspective on our experience, they are also struggling with the class and caste divisions among African-Americans themselves (as well as other "ethnic" Americans). *The Brownies' Book* manifests all of these tensions, often in negative way. For example, in a story entitled, "Impossible Kathleen," author Augusta Bird writes that "Crystal was much the prettier of the two girls. She was just about two shades lighter than Kathleen... Kathleen also knew she was a darker hue than any of the girls in her clique, but she knew she was slenderly built, looked well in all her clothes..." (1920, 10:300) In one of the Judge's columns devoted to a discussion of Americanism, one of the children asserts that he is better than a Chinese American. The Judge invokes insidious notions of class by then posing a hypothetical situation in which men of different nationalities are shipwrecked on an island, asking the young boy, "Suppose not one of you possessed a single thing, which one of you would be the best man?" We can only hope that the readers also heard the Judge when he asked, "Hasn't each of us a right to everything on the island joy, light, love, liberty and the pursuit of happiness?" (1921, 5:134).

It is clear that African-American youngsters (as well as adults) were sorely in need not only of education but of re-education. *The Brownies' Book* itself contained both progressive and problematic information about Africa, especially in reference to Egypt and the "negroness" of its inhabitants. But for the most part, the magazine was concerned with the re-education of its readership, particularly in respect to the very concept of "history." It reveals the ways in which histories are constructed and manipulated and utilized. The editors are aided in this effort by perceptive young readers such as Alice Martin, who offers this shrewd comment on how her school geography book is conceptualized in regard to race:

...all the pictures are pretty, nice-looking men and women, except the Africans. They always look so ugly. I don't mean to make fun of them, for I am not pretty myself; but I know not all colored people look like me. I see lots of ugly white people too; but not all white people look like them, and they are not the ones they put in the geography. (1920, 6:178)

All of this is to say that African-Americans have always been struggling with their own internal tensions while also trying to maintain some sense of "brotherhood" based upon a common heritage and history. And this struggle, so often evident in the pages of *The Brownies' Book*, consistently punctuate the history of African-American children's literature.

In 1932, Langston Hughes (a teenaged contributor to *The Brownies' Book*) and Arna Bontemps published *Popo and Fifina: Children of Haiti* (NY: Macmillan, 1932). This is just one of the first books in this canon of African-American children's literature whose major purpose it is to expose African-American readers to the lives of people in other parts of the African Diaspora. Bontemps' 1948 *The Story of the Negro* (NY: Knopf, 1948), though in strict terms a history book, initiates a continuous line of historical novels set throughout the Diaspora. Lorenz Graham's 1966 *I, Momolu* (NY: Crowell, 1966) is especially notable because of the complexity of the issue that it introduces. Set in Liberia presumably during the 1960s, the book boldly explores the ways in which the society is stratified, whether ethnically, economically, religiously, geographically or linguistically. Momolu, the main character, constantly makes distinctions between the Kewpessie, who are his own people, the Liberians (African-American people of American descent), and other ethnic groups. A multilayered story emerges out of the interweaving of details which give the reader insight into cultural issues food preferences, attitudes toward play and warfare, clothing styles, architecture, religion and missionaries, appropriate codes of adult and child behavior, attitudes toward the past and the future in short, total philosophies of living.

Rosa Guy addresses some of these same issue in *The Friends*, published in 1973 (NY: Bantam). She uses the story of a young West Indian girl not living in New York, to explore, in essence, what happens when the **idea** of brotherhood/sisterhood is tested in real life. What happens when people of African descent, but from various parts of Diaspora, are forced to interact? What is the meaning of "America" to African peoples who choose to migrate here? What is "blackness"? What is "Africanness"? Guy brings into question the significance of Harlem itself in all its mythological stature as home of African-American culture, as well as its sociological standing as an archetypal ghetto. How does place of origin, of birth, define one? What does one's social identity mean in the everyday living of life?

A recent and poignant example of the international context of African-American literature for young people is *Fallen Angels* (NY: Scholastic, 1989) by prolific writer Walter Dean Myers. It is the story of a young African-American who finds himself fighting in Vietnam. Like Myers, who continually returns to the city streets through the pages of his many powerful novels, Richie continually returns to the streets as he analyzes his wartime experience. The army proves to be the environment in which he starkly reexamines his many, many questions, drawing connections, both physical and psychological, between the gang warfare of Harlem and Chicago streets and the Vietnamese fields of war. He draws connections between various peoples of color: confronting a White soldier, he asks, "How come when you say 'gooks' it sounds like 'nigger' to me" (54) He relates feelings of racial unity (not always shared) experienced within a new context: in one particularly incisive episode, a fellow soldier declares, "The way I figure it, we got to stick together over here. I can't trust no whitey to watch my back when the deal go down." (16) To formalize this bond, he suggests that he and fellow African-American soldiers become "blood brothers:" This is symbolic of our common African blood." (16) And finally, Richie constantly questions the meaning of his young life, in both the present and the future. In a seemingly insignificant statement, Myers evokes all of the irony and tragedy of an eighteen-year-old boy going to war: a nurse on Richie's plane to Vietnam "asked me what I wanted to be when I was a kid." (6) One may well ask, who is a youth and who is an adult? What is literature for young people as opposed to literature for adults?

Indeed, this attention to the international and the diasporic is manifest even in the most simple picture books. Lorenz Graham wrote not only young adult novels, but picture books on the same stories. His *Song of the Boat* (NY: Crowell, 1975) is also about Momolu's family. Written in West African pidgin English, it foregrounds issues of language that are relevant on this side of the other side of the Atlantic, too. There is a connecting circle between Graham's books, Ron and Natalie Daise's *The Gullah Storybook*

(Beaufort, S.C.: G.O.G. Enterprises, 1989), Priscilla Jaquith's *Bo Rabbit Smart for True: Folktales from the Gullah* (NY: Pilomel, 1981), and the almost countless retellings of African folklore published in this country.

What is important is that the process of educating African-American youth as people of African descent, as Americans, and as world citizens, is continuing. Furthermore, it is important that this process take place in picture books as well as in young adult books. Counteracting the stereotypes of which DuBois was so acutely aware, and which still exist to an appreciable extent, are the powerful images in books such as Tom Feelings and Muriel Feelings' *Moja Means One: Swahili Counting Book* (NY: Dial, 1971) and *Jambo Means Hello: Swahili Alphabet Book* (NY: Dial, 1974), as well as Leo and Diane Dillon's well-researched paintings in *Ashanti to Zulu: African Traditions* (NY: Dial, 1976).

Especially exciting is a book such as Lucille Clifton's *All Us Come Cross the Water* (NY: Holt, 1973). Its most obvious message is that African-Americans of the "new world" all arrived here together on slave ships and thus share a bond based on their common place of origin. But Clifton's main character goes on to examine this assumption from various perspectives. He brings to task the adults in his life, holding them accountable for remedying their own miseducation and then educating him and his peers. He examines the meaning of his own Swahili name, which is Ujamaa "and that means Unity" (pages unnumbered). He embraces as a brother his friend Bo, whose "Mama is from an island." Ujamaa also understands that all of his friends do not understand, in the intellectual way that he does, what brotherhood is really about. But this realization does not dampen his passion for the significance of the concept itself. *All Us Come Cross the Water* is exciting because it demonstrates that the issues of unity and the diaspora can be explored, even in picture books, without oversimplification to the extent that the ideas become only unrealizable, meaningless ideals.

African-American children's literature is an international literature not solely by force of definition, but because of the conscious and deliberate visions of a succession of writers and artists who from the emerging stages of this canon saw the world as a small place. Most importantly, they saw the world as a place in which words and images together can help people to be honest about who they are in both a personal and social/political, and thus, international context.

African American Folktales Versus White Supremacist Juvenile Fiction

Donnarae MacCann, Ph., D.
University of Iowa, Iowa City, Iowa

Black folktales and white juvenile fiction need to be studied in juxtaposition to one another in 19th century America. The antebellum Euro-American child was being prepared for a domineering social and political role, and the nature of that preparation in mainstream literature supplies clues to modes of discrimination and reinslavement in both the North and South. This negative indoctrination in juvenile fiction required firm opposition from the targeted group: African Americans. Black folktales provided, in some degree, an answer to that propaganda although the tales were often addressing conditions of slavery and race discrimination in the broadest sense.

An important irony is traceable in the postbellum years—a new mix of freedom and bondage. Evidence within children's books shows the scale of indoctrination changing. Freedom from legal slavery resulted in a stepped-up campaign to achieve and sustain extra-legal slavery, a development clearly reflected in books for the young. Euro-American culture presented the doctrine of white superiority in more invidious and multifarious ways.

This essay is about those virulent features in mainstream children's literature, and about the subtle strategies of defense and opposition as seen in Black folktales. Both literatures tell their own political story. To describe works issuing from major publishing houses is to reveal a white supremacist culture that mainstream children were being taught to perpetuate. To describe African American folktales is to illumine a culture of struggle and resistance. This is not to suggest that the literature of either group centered exclusively upon race relations. Black folk literature offered a range of themes and styles, and mainstream children's literature was a multifaceted creative enterprise. But typically the latter presented one message in stories about African American characters—a message implying the innate inferiority of Blacks.

The Literature of "White Supremacy"

The myth of white superiority is present even in the books written by *anti*-slavery proponents—Northern educators and journalists who were close to the "liberal" end of the political spectrum. The entrenchment of that myth in even these "progressive" forces provides a clue to the mainstream's social and economic arrangements for ex-slaves, arrangements that produced conditions increasingly inhumane as well as unequal.

Jacob Abbott is an example of an influential New England educator, a man who eventually became known as "the father of the story series." (Jordan, 78) His children's novel, *Congo, or Jasper's Experience in Command* (1857), proclaims African American inferiority in straightforward, didactic terms, although the surface treatment of Congo is cordial. Genteel manners pervade the texture of the narrative, but the "kindness" expressed by the protagonists toward Congo (a free Black teenager) is accompanied by authorial messages to the readership—messages that stereotype Blacks in the worst way. For example, when a white farmer wishes to teach his grandson, Jasper, the art of entrepreneurship, he instructs him to employ Congo as his laborer; then he generalizes about Congo's character:

> "I think [Congo] is likely to spend his life as a laborer, or perhaps as a coachman or footman in some gentleman's family. Such a kind of life as that is the one that he is best qualified for, and that is undoubtedly what he would like the best. It is one of the characteristics of the colored people to like to be employed by other people, rather than to take

responsibility and care upon themselves." (102)

The stereotyping continues as Grandfather warns Jasper away from any serious effort to teach Congo basic skills:

> "I don't think I would do that [teach Congo to write]. You see, in attempting to teach him to write, you don't expect he will ever make much of a penman. All you can hope for is that he will learn to write his name and make figures, so as to calculate an account or something of that sort." (104)

A rhetorical device that is typical in books of this sort is the affirmation of inferiority from the African American characters themselves. Thus Congo himself rejects the idea of learning to write, and the reader will probably see this decision as appropriate since Congo is portrayed throughout as a lesser human being than Jasper. When the boys are in a burning building, for example, Congo is "ready to faint with terror" and "is almost beside himself," whereas Jasper is a model of courage, composure, and the ability to take command. (155-156) Congo is so totally dependent upon his Anglo-Saxon counterpart that readers may well feel relief when Congo is safely placed in the care of Jasper's mother at the end of the tale. We have seen no normal capacity in Congo to mature, excel, or identify himself outside the routine realm of servitude. He becomes, therefore, the family coachman.

Jacob Abbott's position toward slavery was one shared in many "respectable" circles in pre-war New England—namely, that slavery be left alone in the South, but prohibited from extension into the new West. This was the policy Abbott taught his son, Lyman, urging him to become a lawyer and follow the right way to "strike . . . a blow for liberty," rather than become an activist in Kansas' fight to be a free-soil state. (Lyman Abbott, 98)

In discussions about the slave status of Washington, D.C., the senior Abbott recommended the abolition of slavery in that ten square mile area. He said forced labor within the District was "entirely inconsistent with the theoretical principles which this nation advances." (Quinlivan, 29) He failed to see the lameness of his logic. How on earth could conformity to democratic principles in one tiny geographical space compensate for the denial of those principles in the rest of the South?

There is clearly an ambivalence in Abbott and it becomes easier to understand when we look at his writings for children. His son called him a political radical, but his messages to the young reveal a firm belief in the inherent rightness of white domination and its correlative, the exploitation of African Americans.[1]

John Townsend Trowbridge was another Northerner, another "liberal," one who attempted a direct attack upon the institution of slavery in his children's novel *Cudjo's Cave* (1864). In childhood Trowbridge was taught the same policy position as Abbott's son: that the line against slavery should be held in the new Western territories. But he became a fervent abolitionist as he watched slave-catchers operating aggressively in New England following the 1850 Fugitive Slave Act. Still, his anti-slavery stance was contradicted in *Cudjo's Cave* by a heavy use of "blackface" minstrel and "savage" stereotypes. For the historian, Trowbridge is a prime example of surface attitudes undergoing change, while at a basic level impressions about race remain unchanged.

A review of the Black characters in this long, intricate novel will be enough to suggest the nature of Trowbridge's ambivalence toward Blacks. The heroic "Pomp" voiced many anti-slavery arguments, but Trowbridge makes his nobility dependent upon contact with a white master. When the master dies suddenly, leaving his servant still enslaved, the bereaved Pomp flees to a mountain cave where he lives with "Cudjo." The latter is a runaway who was so violently abused by a plantation overseer that he has reverted to the so-called bestial status of his African ancestors. He has "a body like a frog's and the countenance of an ape . . . more like a demon . . . than a human being . . . petulant and malicious . . ." (118, 119, 123) While Pomp is generally portrayed as an intelligent, compassionate individual, the author indicates that even he is sometimes on the brink of relapsing to a so-called primitive state. At the novel's climax, a white woman teaches Pomp compassion when he is about to become brutish; ("in [Pomp's] face shone a persuasive glitter of the old, untamable, torrid ferocity of his tribe . . ."). (468)

"Toby," the former slave of a Southern family, is the most minstrel-like character. He struts, boasts, and frequently changes a word such as "reconnoiter" to "reconoyster," and "carbonic acid" to "carbunkum asses." He is free, but could obviously not survive without close supervision; he possesses a "large tropical heart" but "a foolish head." He functions as a male "mammy" figure, remaining in the service of his old master and donating his life-savings so the family can flee from the war. As he digs up the money, he reveals his misunderstanding of what wages and self-determination are all about:

> "Gold sar! Gold, Miss Jinny! Needn't look 'spicious!
> I neber got 'em by no underground means!" (He
> meant to say *underhand*) . . . Ye see, Massa Villars,
> eber sence ye gib me my freedom, ye been payin' me
> right smart wages,—seben dollar a monf! . . . An'
> you rec'lec' you says to me, you says, "Hire it out
> to some honest man, Toby, and ye kin draw infer-
> ence on it," you says. (494)

Toby then refuses any expressions of thanks, saying that "Massa" has only himself to thank because it was his idea to give Toby money. Toby sees the wages as a gift rather than as compensation for labor.

While Trowbridge does swing back and forth from a somewhat radicalized post-1850 mood to the use of the "stage Negro" tradition, he was unable to relinquish the white supremacy myth. Portraiture in *Cudjo's Cave* is imbued with that myth, despite the author's goal to do his "own humble part in [the Civil War]," to write a book "frankly designed to fire the Northern heart" (as he says in *My Own Story*). (262)

The postbellum Northern heart, including its accelerating penchant for racist children's literature, is visible in the pages of *St. Nicholas Magazine*. This widely acclaimed publication began in 1873 under the editorship of Mary Mapes Dodge, a member of the Northern genteel Establishment. Dodge recruited well-respected and often well-known writers, sold her magazine to 70,000 subscribers, and began in *St. Nicholas* an "institution" with extraordinary influence—a publication that lasted until 1939 and was then anthologized to extend its influence for another generation.

Many stories could be cited as illustrations of the *St. Nicholas* attitude toward African Americans. For example, "A Funny Little School" is a work that includes the theme of Black uneducability. This story by Ruth McEnery Stuart features an African American cast with five elderly men, a dim-witted woman, and a twelve-year-old who agrees to teach all the others to read. Almost every scene reads like a "blackface" minstrel skit. The child's grandfather is one of the "scholars" and delivers a monologue about "dat big A," a letter that "sort o' looks like my ole 'oman." (372) Another class member suspects unfair treatment when his name is not part of the lesson. Like a spoiled child he complains: "I done tooken notice dat Tom an' Sol been spelt a week ago, an' it's a' outrage dat I ain't been spelt long ago." (375) The teacher complains about everyone's "ignunce," but she is clearly an unteachable student herself, even unsure about the alphabet she is explaining.

The so-called humor of "blackface," the exaggerated quarreling, boasting, swaggering, fabricating, and improvising on the English language—these are all regular features in *St. Nicholas* stories. But in the post-Reconstruction era (the period when *St. Nicholas* began publication) something stronger than ridicule was served up to children. The clowning is coupled with more malicious aspersions on African American character, as when a youngster's mother and sister are portrayed as child-abusers, thieves, and drunks in Clara Morris's "My Little 'Jim Crow'." Northern whites, the employers of this group, are presented as the kindly saviors of the mistreated child.

Euro-Americans are often contrasted with African Americans and presented as the antidote to the havoc created by the latter. In other stories, the white supremacy theme is underscored by the way the Blacks are made to idolize Anglo-Saxons. Such reverence pervades Ruth McEnery Stuart's "An Old-Time Christmas Gift," a story that revolves around the idea of an eternal master/slave relationship. In this narrative, Yuyu, (a slave and later an ex-slave) is seen placing her head beneath the hand of her child-mistress and declaring her wish for a life-long status as a personal servant. Even though slavery has ended, the gesture of hand-on-head is explained by Yuyu: "It mean dat I 's yo' little nigger, an' you's my little mistus—dat what it mean. *Lay it on.*" (102)

The different means for implying white superiority are too numerous to present in detail, but we need to note that this feature in *St. Nicholas* did not lessen the magazine's prestige in mainstream circles. In 1948 the well-known historian Henry Steele Commager included Stuart's "A Funny Little School" in an anthology of *St. Nicholas* stories—selections that Commager labeled "the best." (xxi) His unstinting praise for that story and others suggests that the socializing power of children's reading materials is indeed great—greater than Commager's training in history could counteract.

The Black community could not overcome the continuing abusiveness of Euro-American children's literature nor diminish its popularity with whites, but it could create its own art. This it has never failed to do since the beginnings of slavery in the Western Hemisphere. The political implications in much of that art was a counter to the political indoctrination from mainstream sources. African American folk art was a means of defense for adults and children alike, albeit the form of that art was of necessity subtle (even undecipherable to the slave-owning class). The allegory and animal fable made their points indirectly.

Black Folktales: A Strong Defense

In 1888, William Wells Newell, editor of the *Journal of American Folk-Lore,* made a prophecy about Black folktales. In his review of Charles C. Jones's *Negro Myths from the Georgia Coast* (1888), Newell wrote: "A century hence, the people [of Georgia and the Carolinas] will be thankful for the care which has preserved tradition which they will then regard as precious." (169) Today this prophecy is largely confirmed; modern folklorists generally regard Black folk literature as a valuable expression of folk art.

As an embodiment of a communal system—as a crystallization of the thoughts and sensibilities of the African American masses— these tales surely reached children. Moreover, the stories probably served Black children as at least a partial remedy for white supremacist propaganda. The stories are instructive metaphors about how to cope with racism and how to sustain a strong sense of self-worth.

The tales described below are examples that have political ramifications, although many other types of tales were also created by the folk. The stories are from 19th century publications, and since the collectors usually described their sources as slaves, we can assume that the tales date from both the ante- and postbellum eras.

We need to digress briefly to consider an unfortunate irony within these published versions of the narratives, an irony that connects them with the biased postbellum political milieu. Put succinctly, it is ironic that 19th century publications included a dialect that has itself been described as an attack upon Black culture. By taking an authentic literature and presenting it in an inauthentic tongue, the mainstream publishing world managed to weaken the themes and give the stories an association with the "blackface" theater. Still, the messages are too strong to be lost, and 19th century Black audiences undoubtedly heard many of the stories orally and without the distorting dialect of the printed page. As we examine the stories, we need to keep the dialect problem in mind, an issue that does not concern speech patterns *per se,* but concerns the distortion of speech for political ends.

The problem, stated briefly, is that a double standard was applied to local color dialects for white characters and the dialects ascribed to Blacks. Folklorist Harold Courlander writes:

> The speech of whites normally was represented in traditional orthography, even though some of them pronounced various words much the same as did the blacks. (258)

Thus in folktales included in Joel Chandler Harris's "Uncle Remus" stories, an "eye dialect" was invented—an incorrect spelling intended to suggest an inferior level of intelligence. Euro-American characters said "was" and Black characters said "wuz"; "been" became "bin," "lizard" became "lizzud," "measles" became "meezles," "husband" became "huzbin'" and so on. Courlander refers to such excesses in spelling and to the grammatical misconstructions that often accompanied them as a form of social abuse.

He further notes that this treatment of dialect often overshadowed the content and meaning of a story. The white readership may have enjoyed this additional form of ridicule and its links with the "blackface" tradition, but the effect on children was disastrous. Prejudice was reinforced in white children, and African American children became ashamed of a great literature. As Alice M. Bacon of the Hampton Folk-Lore Society reported in 1897, "it is almost impossible for [teachers in the public schools] to gather from their pupils any folk-lore at all, so certain are they, if they have any, that it is something only to be laughed at . . ."[2] (17)

Thus the Black child faced a double dilemma: the racist mainstream literature and the inauthentic, demeaning dialects in written versions of Black folk literature. Fortunately, when the children heard the tales in an authentic oral form, they received a refutation of a white supremacist ideology.

That ideology is countered in *Negro Myths from the Georgia Coast*, especially when tales present an intuitive awareness of power struggles. For example, in "Buh Goat and Buh Wolf," Goat and his wife are so frightened by thunder and lightning that they beg Buh Wolf for shelter in his house. Wolf gladly escorts them into his shed, locks the door, and is so giddy about his sudden luck that he sings this song:

"Tenky goolly God, tunder and lightnin done sen

meat een me house." (153)

Wolf's wife warns him to keep still or the goats will get suspicious and escape. When Wolf ignores her, the goats do dig a hole and run off. Later Goat meets Wolf and the latter is offended:

> "Buh Goat, wuh sort er mean trick dat wuh you bin do be dis mornin?"

Buh Goat, him bex, an him mek answer:

> "How you hab de face fuh talk long me an ax me sich er question? Enty you bin fix fuh kill me an me wife dis mornin arter you done gie we de freedom er you house?" (153)

Wolf threatens to pick his bones straight away next time, but Goat says he won't get the chance because Goat will always keep an eye on him.

As in most of the tales, the precepts in this one are never made explicit, but the action carries several warnings: Don't flee from a small danger to a large one; don't be off guard just because someone makes hospitable gestures (even giving you "de freedom er [his/her] house") don't give an enemy a second chance (from "dat day tel dis," Goat watched Wolf suspiciously).

Another tale about power relationships is "When Brer Frog Give a Big Dining," a story published in the *Journal of American Folk-Lore* in 1900 and retold by Emma M. Backus. Brer Frog represents the "underdog," being the smallest, and Brer Rabbit is the exploiter who comes to a bad end. (In some tales, a creature such as a frog, snail, or partridge serves as a stand-in for a slave, while Brer Rabbit—who is so often a slave symbol—is the symbol of the slavemaster.) As the story begins, it is explained that "there be hard feelings between Brer Frog and Brer Rabbit from way back." (25) Thus Rabbit is not invited to Frog's fish fry. He manages, nonetheless, to break in on the party, scare off all the guests, and gorge himself. Frog is able to watch the acts of vandalism because his eyes are on the top of his head and the rest of him is hidden in the water. So Frog conspires his revenge by announcing a second party and arranging the table so it will fall into the water when Rabbit begins eating. Then he gives Rabbit a piece of his mind before he "eat him up": "You is my master many a day on land, Brer Rabbit, but I is your master in the water." (25)

In short, you may have to fight, even when your cause is just and warrants a peaceful solution; but try to stage the battle on your own homeground.

A variation on such tactical maneuvers is presented in "Brer Rabbit Beats Brer Fox," a story about rendering people vulnerable by beating them at their own game. First a squirrel, who is always a copycat, is lured into danger when Brer Fox says: "I once had a brother who could jump from limb to limb." Squirrel says, "So can I." The pattern is repeated when Fox says from "tree to tree" and then switches his boast to include a jump "into my arms." The last jump is squirrel's undoing. But that is not the end. Brer Rabbit, who has been watching all this, picks up the trickery with these words to Brer Fox:

> "My brother could let anybody tie a large rock around his neck, and jump off this bridge into the water and swim out." ("Folklore Scrapbook," 229-230)

After his successes, Fox is now brash and unwary. He chimes in: "So can I" and he hasn't been heard from since!

In the famous "Tar Baby" story there are political implications that have been eliminated from most re-tellings. Typically, the tale is one of reverse psychology: Rabbit challenging a tar baby, getting stuck, and then shrewdly managing to end up in his own brier patch. In A.M.H. Christensen's version in *Afro-American Folk Lore* (1892), there is a more extensive battle of wits between Rabbit and Wolf. Rabbit takes Wolf's corn one year and his peanut crop the next; he knocks down Wolf's scarecrow, then becomes stuck to Wolf's tar baby, but tricks Wolf into throwing him into the brier patch. Later Rabbit is almost tricked when Wolf plays dead and lures Rabbit to his funeral. But Rabbit discovers the deception and is "one-up" on Wolf when he puts a dab of snuff on the supposed corpse's nose, causing Wolf to sneeze. (62)

In the first two sentences, the narrator offers the basic theme: "Wolf 'e bery wise man . . . but de Rabbit 'e mos' cunnin' man dat go on four leg." The competition here is between slavemaster and slave and is illustrated by tricks at different levels of sophistication. The "thieving" is explained by the fact that Wolf has planted corn, but Rabbit has planted nothing at all. (As actually a slave, Rabbit <u>could not</u> plant and the listeners know this although the point is left unstated.) In the series of tricks, Rabbit first escapes from a fairly unsophisticated trap: a scarecrow, which he simply knocks down. But mere force does not work on the more deceptive trap, the tar baby, who is shaped like a Black woman in this story. Her silence, after Rabbit cordially asks, "Gal, wha' you name?" exasperates Rabbit and he hits and kicks until he is stuck in five places. But the reverse psychology then works on Wolf, and Wolf is so mad that he sends Dog to invite Rabbit to his funeral. Rabbit is wary of both Dog (Wolf's relative) and Mrs. Wolf and escapes from the clutches of the mock corpse.

At least two political messages are apparent in this version of "tar baby": first, if one is "the most cunning man on four legs," the more sophisticated forms of entrapment will be understood, and second, it is well to treat intermediaries with utmost caution.

These stories about power illustrate the importance of wisdom and wit in what is essentially a political arena. Themes pertaining to courage, fairness, family solidarity, the work ethic, and other valuable principles are also abundantly present in Black folklore and make this lore an important aid in the socialization of children. Moreover, "there is a wide, wide wonder in it all"—a phrase coined by James Weldon Johnson in relation to African American spirituals but equally descriptive of the tales.

Conclusion

Returning to William Wells Newell's review of *Negro Myths . . .*, we find his assertion that "even the lore of children may become an important part of history,—quite as important as records of elections and political activity." (170) As an editor of a scholarly folklore journal, Newell was perhaps unconscious of the degree to which children's literature *was* "political activity." But by putting the white supremacist stories side by side with their antidote in Black culture, the significance of juvenile books as part of the total political record becomes clear.

Our studies in the field of children's literature should reflect that reality. Children represent the future, and their elders busily prepare them for a political role in that future. Artists may well be the more influential elders since they entertain while they enlighten; in any case, there can be little doubt that they interpret the world as they describe it. To analyze quality in art means that our focus will include the complex social and political contexts of literature—whether in our own time or in the past.

Notes

1. Mary E. Quinlivan argues in *The Journal of Popular Culture* (Summer, 1982) that Abbott was quite a liberal, as proven by his "Rainbow" books. This series about a Black teenager called "Rainbow" expresses, in my view, the same hierarchy of Euro-American over African American that is noticeable in *Congo* . . . "Rainbow" is developed more fully, but his inferior condition in the novels is stereotypic.

2. Because the printed dialect was such a distortion, William Wells Newell urged a halt in dialect manuscripts for his *Journal of American Folk-Lore*. In explanation he wrote:

> It is obviously impossible by means of the regular alphabet to reproduce negro dialect with any accuracy. A phonetic alphabet is essential for such purpose. . . The attempt to indicate the manner of enunciation by the usual English signs results in confusions and contradictions innumerable . . . An equally serious fault is that the meaning and real interest of the tale is disguised; a dialectic story is apt to be a mere piece of jargon, in which the lack of deep human interest is atoned for by a spelling which is usually mere affectation. (*Journal of American Folk-Lore*, Vol. 11, 1889, pp. 291-292.)

"Black English," as we define it today, is not to be equated with the 19th century printed dialects.

Works Cited

Abbott, Jacob. *Congo: Or, Jasper's Experience in Command*. New York: Harper & Brothers, 1857.

Abbott, Lyman. *Reminiscences*. Boston: Houghton, Mifflin Co., 1915.

Bacon, Alice M. "Work and Methods of the Hampton Folk-Lore Society," *Journal of American Folk-Lore*, 11 (1898).

Backus, Emma M. "Folktales from Georgia," *Journal of American Folk-Lore*, 13 (January-March, 1900).

Christensen, A.M.H. *Afro-American Folk Lore; Told Round Cabin on the Sea Islands of South Carolina*. New York: Negro Universities Press, 1969; originally published by J.G. Cupples Co. in Boston, 1892.

Commager, Henry Steele, ed. *The St. Nicholas Anthology*. New York: Random House, 1948.

Courlander, Harold. *A Treasury of Afro-American Folklore*. New York: Crown Publishers, 1976.

"Folklore Scrapbook," *Journal of American Folk-Lore*, 12 (January-March 1899).

Jones, Charles C. *Negro Myths from the Georgia Coast*. Columbia, S.C.: The State Co., 1925; originally published in 1888.

Jordan, Alice M. "The Children of Jacob Abbott," in *From Rollo to Tom Sawyer and Other Papers*. Boston: The Horn Book, Inc., 1948.

Morris, Clara. "My Little 'Jim Crow'," *St. Nicholas Magazine* 26:2 (December, 1898).

Newell, William Wells. "Books," *Journal of American Folk-Lore*, 1 (April-June, 1888).

Quinlivan, Mary E. "Race Relations in the Ante-bellum Children's Literature of Jacob Abbott," *Journal of Popular Culture* 16:1 (Summer, 1982).

Stuart, Ruth McEnery. "A Funny Little School," *St. Nicholas Magazine*, 25:1 (November, 1897).

____. "An Old Time Christmas Gift," *St. Nicholas Magazine*, 25:2 (December, 1897).

Trowbridge, John Townsend. *Cudjo's Cave*. Boston: J.E. Tilton & Co., 1864.

____. *My Own Story: With Recollections of Noted Persons*. Boston: Houghton, Mifflin and Co., 1903.

Multiculturalism and Theater for African-American Youth in the '90s

Michele McNichols, Ph. D.
Clark Atlanta University

Introduction

The provocative and troubling aspect of attempting to describe viable theater for African American youth is that so much of what is to be said is applicable to viable theater for all youth - and even to all theater. Much of theater - for adults as well as for youth would benefit from the incorporation of the practices and processes identified with desirable theater for African American youth. So, while describing appropriate theater for African American youth seems to suggest that those characteristics are appropriate ONLY for African American youth, nothing could be further from the truth.

So why write this article? Why read it? Well, the fact is, that, of course, all cultures have characteristics that appear in all aspects of that culture. Language, both verbal and non-verbal, the way language is used, the intonations, the accompanying body language, the number of words used for the same generic thing, (ie. snow), the quantity of verbal language used, the manner in which communication occurs, are often distinct in differing cultures.

Add to that, matters of food and food preparation, social relations, child rearing, religion, dress, governance and of course, the arts.

People in different cultures often have varying senses of what is desirable and good in art. We have different aesthetics. While ideals in aesthetics are modified over time, what probably actually modifies a cultural aesthetic is interaction with another culture. But culture is tenacious. So it comes to be that a large number of the descendents of enslaved Africans who were brought to this country hundreds of years ago, and whose culture was assaulted in an astonishing variety of ways, are still carriers of many aspects of that culture. And for theatre for the youth of that culture to be effective - for it to touch, move, expand thinking -the African American aesthetic must be honored.

Much has been written about the African American aesthetic. What will be done here, is simply to remind readers of some of the admonitions of the revolutionary Black theatre artists of the l960's, to discuss the relevance of their thinking and work to the nineties concept of "multiculturalism," and to discuss some implications for anyone creating or performing theatre for and/or with African American youth in the l990's.

Multiculturalism

In this era when "multiculturalism" is a buzzword, and earnest middle class citizens of all cultural groups take pride in the ability to function comfortably, knowledgeably and sensitively in differing cultural environments, there may actually be a growing appreciation of aesthetics other than one's own. Members of any society's subordinate groups (those who come up short in the arenas
of power, privilege, prestige and wealth), have always been at least bicultural, in that they can communicate, function and survive in the culture of the dominant group. A growing number of middle class citizens find that while appreciation of the culture of "others" is not critical to immediate survival, appreciation can enhance and enrich life. Some also recognize that a two way avenue of cultural appreciation may increase chances of survival for all of us, globally.

Many African Americans, though, are highly suspicious of the concept of "multiculturalism." Assuming achievement of the goals of multiculturalism, what we would have, they say, would be yet another way of diluting and distorting the importance of African American culture. They say that, especially in school systems in which the large majority of students are African American, (systems in most of our urban centers), what is needed is a radical revision of the curriculum to focus on African American culture and contributions. The curriculum has been dominated by Euro-centric attitudes and perspectives for too long, it is argued; information critical to the cultural and racial self respect of African American youth has been omitted from texts and teaching for too long, for redress to occur by inserting a "unit" on African Americans, along with units on Asian Americans, Native Americans, Irish Americans, ad infinitum. Without dismissing the validity of these arguments, though, it is also true that there are some convergences between the goals of multiculturalism and the goals of the revolutionary Black theatre artists of the 1960's.

Part of the difficulty in discussing "multiculturalism" is that, as with the terms "integration" in the fifties and "affirmative action" in the sixties, the term "multiculturalism" means different things to different people. Some see it as a promotion of an amalgamation of cultures that will render us all homogeneous. The chances of that happening may be measured by the success of the decades old artificial language Esperanto, the so-called "universal" language, which all citizens of the world were going to learn to speak in order to communicate without the inconvenience of language differences. How many among this article's readers know Esperanto?

Some suggest that "multiculturalism" is simply an updated term for the old "melting pot" ideal. Today it is recognized that the "melting pot" ideal referred to the degree to which those with other than English or Northern European heritages could adopt the language and other cultural characteristics of the dominant group. The degree of success of the real "melting pot" ideal then, is the degree to which those not of European heritage have adopted the language, customs, styles and manners of the dominant European culture. Many have, but, decades after the coining of the "melting pot" phrase, a new catchword, the "unmeltables," was coined to describe those who those who either could not or would not conform.

Yet another way of thinking of "multiculturalism" is that it refers to cultural pluralism. In a culturally pluralistic society, no one cultural group is dominant, and all groups are valued equally. People are aware of and appreciative of the styles and values of cultures other than their own. To continue the use of terms from sociology, a culturally pluralistic interpretation of multiculturalism infers a "mixed salad" society, with all cultures retaining individuality, yet functioning as a part of a harmonious whole. A recognition of and respect for a variety of cultural aesthetics would exist, as would a variety of standards for aesthetic criticism. Artists who consciously chose to use their art as conveyers of their cultural identities would heighten the cultural aspects of their work, and could expect and would get appreciation for working toward the goals of their own cultural aesthetic.

This "new criticism" is one that even many artists within the same cultural group have often sought. "Find out what I was TRYING to do, before you critique me," they say. " How can you decide whether I was successful or not if you don't even know what I was trying to achieve?" This plea is the highly compatible with the concepts of the revolutionary Black theatre artists of the 1960's, those who followed closely the Black Nationalist musicians, and several of whom created work relevant in both genres (Amiri Baraka, Archie Schepp). The anger of these theatre artists at being judged by cultural standards other than their own was so strong that their challenge became to ignore the dominant standards of theatre criticism in order to rediscover their own cultural aesthetic and to communicate exclusively for African Americans.

The Black Theatre Revolution

In the 1960's in America, the society as a whole, and thus the society of theatre and of theatre criticism, was even further from being culturally pluralistic than it is now. Images of African Americans in theatre had moved from the ludicrous representations of minstrelsy of the 1860's, '70s and '80s, through the Creole shows and "coon shows" of the turn of the century. The images had shifted to those of the "Brute Negro . . . a black Beast given to rape, pillage, and murder" in the early 1900's (Hatch 1972, 10), and the "Exotic Primitive," as exemplified by Eugene O'Neill's Emperor Jones (Hatch 1972, 11). The mid-1930's produced the "Negro" theatre branch of the Federal Theatre Project in which European Americans frequently wrote for and directed African Americans. By as late as 1949, Langston Hughes could still write:

> "You put me in MACBETH and CARMEN JONES
> And all kinds of SWING MIKADOS
> And in everything but what's about me -
> But someday somebody'll
> Stand up and talk about me
> And write about me -
> Black and beautiful -
> And sing about me,
> And put on plays about me!

I reckon it'll be
Me myself!

Yes, it'll be me."
(Hughes 1979, 190)

For the most part, images of African Americans on the popular stage were still being created by and for European Americans. African American performers who participated in "classical" performance, were committed to a European repertoire, and thus they too functioned within an aesthetic which emerged out of a heritage not their own.

But by the 1960's, Langston Hughes' "me" was ready to take over.

Don L. Lee, as quoted by Larry Neal in a 1968 article, said, "It's time for DuBois, Nat Turner, and Kwame Nkrumah. As Franz Fanon points out: destroy the culture and you destroy the people. This must not happen." (Neal 1968, 29)   He quotes Maulana Karenga:

"Without a culture Negroes are only a set of reactions to white people." And he quotes Amiri Baraka: "The Revolutionary Theatre should force change. It should be change." (Neal 1968, 33)

Revolutionary playwrights exhorted their colleages to "go home aesthetically." (King and Milner 1971, viii) In a 1969 interview, Ed Bullins said, "Black people had to come together and create our own theatre . . . . We don't want to have a higher form of white art in black-face. We are working toward something entirely different and new that encompasses the soul and spirit of Black people, and that represents the whole experience of our being here in this oppressive land." (Bullins 1969, ix & xii) Woodie King and Ron Milner went on: "Black theatre is, in fact about the destruction of tradition, the traditional role of Negroes in white theatre." (King and Milner 1971, viii)

African American theatre artists of the 1960's burst through old restrictions. They no longer allowed themselves to be defined by Whites, and, in large numbers, gave up the attempt to emulate European derived theatre. In a whirlwind search for personal and ethnic identity, they began to write for, direct for, and speak for and to Blacks. Rather than copying the style, content and form of White theatre, Blacks searched for style, content and form compatible with an African heritage and appropriate for expression of the African American experience.

Carlton Molette, a member of the "New Black Theatre" vanguard, said:

> "One of the highest priority items among those of us who are concerned with the history, theory, and criticism of Afro-American theatre is a redefinition of Afro-American theatre, within the framework of the Afro-American culture. We must not continue to accept a Euro-centric concept of what constitutes a good play, or a bad play, how an audience ought to behave, and so on. If we do, we will never even begin to discover the vast and beautiful and exciting history of our own theatre."
> (Jeyifous 1974, 34)

The African American Aesthetic

What is the aesthetic of which these revolutionary theatre artists spoke and wrote so vehemently? That question must be addressed before one can contemplate how that aesthetic can shape theatre for youth. Key to the answer is in an understanding of the performer/audience relationship. A better way to say it is that, traditionally, the distinction between audience and performers does not exist. As in ancient ritual, there is no real division between audience and performers. All are participants. Participants have differing roles, and those roles vary, with different people assuming leadership, but all are participants. This basic perspective radically affects the nature of the performance experience. Performance is a communal affair, and audience members participate freely. They often show interest by making comments to the performers over the course of the performance, and by showing support or distain for characters by calling out advice, cautions or criticisms. Hoots, hollers and other non-verbal comments are common.

As in African American children's games, and as in jazz, improvisation within the context of the group is characteristic. A good example of how this tradition functions is to experience African American children's games such as "Zoodio", "Aunt Dinah's Dead" or "Punchinella." In all of these games, everyone plays all the time, but the leadership changes. The "featured" participants get to improvise as creatively and imaginatively as they wish, within the rhythm of the chant, with rhythmic chanting and clapping supporting their efforts. Individual embellishment is admired and supported when done within the context of the community effort.

A fact that contributes to improvisation, is the oral nature of recording events and teaching others. Since the African tradition is oral, there is freedom for those who retell the "story," to adjust it in each telling to suit the current audience, mood and time. An accurate feel for the audience contributes to rich interaction with that audience and enhances the appropriateness of improvisation.

Complex rhythm patterns often form the structure for games, as well as for jazz, and the rhythm patterns are most often stated percussively, reminiscent of the functional importance of the drum in African cultures. In games, percussion is achieved through clapping, stomping and striking of the body, as in "James Brown," and in "Hambone." Underlying rhythm acts as a backbone to which one is always attached, so that even in the most extravagant of improvisations, there is something to keep one from flying out in space, lost forever. Rhythmic structure is both a place to come home to and a way to get there, when one has exhausted the possibilities of one's embellishment.

Call and response, a staple of the African American church, is embedded in the cultural style, and is evident in children's games, in music and in conversational patterns. The leader asks a question, or makes a comment, and the congregation responds. Even within the context of a sermon being given for the first time, there are pauses where the congregation knows it is time to comment. African American audiences, frequently having had training in the call and response pattern for much of their lives, often employ it in the theatre experience.

Theater for African American Youth in the '90's

Have the concepts of the Black Theater movement of the 1960's and the ideals of the African aesthetic impacted on theater for African American youth of the 1990's? Certainly not in any overwheming way. Theater for youth is often seen as peripheral to "real" theater, anyway. A "cutesy-pie" approach to "Kiddie Theater" is all too common. And, except for enlightened theater companies, such as Academy Theater in Atlanta, Georgia; Atlanta Street Theater, also in Atlanta; Carpetbag Theater in Knoxville, Tennessee; Crossroads Theater in New Brunswick, New Jersey; Living Stage in Washington, D. C., the matter of cultural style and the aesthetic sense of audience members is of no concern.

When a performing group is brought in from Brazil, or Ghana, there is often much made of the style of performance common to that culture. But when an African American group appears before a primarily European American audience, the educational opportunity inherent in the occasion is usually overlooked. There is, of course, no need to educate non-European American audiences to the European aspects of performance, since the European aesthetic dominates American popular culture.

What enlightened theater companies have done, to greater or lesser extents, and with greater and lesser conscious awareness as to the African American aesthetic, points the way to what others can do. And the ways in which African American theater aesthetic can be evidenced in the work of theater companies can be enumerated.

As in African American children's games and as in jazz, the productions themselves rely on an ensemble of performers, rather than a "star," supported by a cast of actors who serve primarily as background for the star. Many performers are featured over the course of the play, with the ensemble serving to support whichever of them is being featured at the moment.

There is significant interaction and participation with and by audience members in a variety of ways, and audience members may affect the course of action of the play. The entire audience may participate in activities proscribed by the play itself (becoming a forest, creating the sounds of a storm); the audience may be implored to help characters at different points in the play ("They're after me. Somebody, please help me, somehow."); audience members may join the actors in the performing areas (to complete an onstage team for some effort integral to the play); or they may be asked to make decisions about the direction of the course of the play ("What should I do now?"). They certainly may sing, clap and participate at appropriate times.

Significant audience participation requires improvisational responses on the part of the performers, and so, as in other aspects of the African American culture, improvisation abounds. Improvisation with audience members during a play requires flexibility and quick thinking on the part of the performers. Actors can take risks in their improvisations because they know that they will be supported by the rest of the performing ensemble. There is a community of people working toward the same goal, and a structure within which they are working. That structure is the place to come home to and the ensemble will help the performer find the way home. Additionally, a skilled company elicits supportive participation from audiences because it knows how to involve audiences as contributing members of a temporary community.

In theatre springing out of the African aesthetic, music, rhythm, chant and movement are integral to performance. Musicians are on stage, as opposed to being hidden in an orchestra pit, and actors often serve in the dual capacities of actor and musician. Both music and movement serve to carry forth the action of the play, as opposed to providing interludes in the action.

The working style of companies functioning within the African American aesthetic has certain characteristics which will also be evident in its training programs for youth. Work will tend to be collaborative, with companies often creating their own new work, either with or without a director. If there is a playwright, that playwright will often work with company members to write the play. The playwright may ask the performers to take on the role of particular characters and then improvise a situation. Or the playwright may bring scenes that have been written the previous night, for actors to try out in rehearsal, with the thought that there will be rewriting. Music, dance and improvisation will be integral to the development of work, rather than being tacked on later, and the entire piece will evolve out of a communal process.

The characteristics described above are by no means typical only of African American theatre companies performing for African American youth. In fact, some of the styles of working described are typical of dozens of predominantly White theatres throughout the country, and the world, during the 1960's and 1970's. Additionally, within the history of Western theatre, there are many examples of companies which worked collaboratively, or with which audiences interacted vigorously. Conversely, there are currently African American theatre companies for both adults and youth whose work is almost totally outside of the African American aesthetic.

It is also true that, at this point, in the United States, some of us have borrowed so extensively from each other's cultures, that what seems second nature to us, may actually be derived from somewhere other than our own cultural heritage. Certainly, not all African Americans exhibit all of the characteristics attributable to the culture, and they certainly are not exhibited all of the time. In fact, many African Americans could teach everyone else what it means to be multicultural, in the sense of being able to function effectively within several different cultures. And just as certainly, other Americans exhibit some of these characteristics of the African American culture.

Consider many of our young people's preferred styles of music, dress and language, for example.

But there are attributes, merely a few of which are described here, which together form a constellation of characteristics that are typical of many of the observable phenomenom of the African American culture. They show up in theatre, music, dance, literature, conversation, games, rituals, ceremonies, dress, language. To bring relevant and effective theatre to African American youth, and to involve them in meaningful ways in theatre activities, we must be cognizant of their cultural styles, and we must value and honor those styles.

Conclusion

It is hard enough to be a European American adolescent today; it is infinitely harder still, to be an African American adolescent. The challenges and confusion are quite obviously overwhelming to many. Those of us in theater have at our disposal a tool that can make a difference. Theater is power. Unlike any other medium, unlike any other institution, theater can involve the hearts and minds of audiences in vicariously living through what real people on stage are portraying. That experience can expand awareness of what the consequences of various choices are, of what it sometimes takes to succeed in an effort, of what it means to be human. No lecture has the potential power of effective theater.

Theater is also a tool of power for young people to use themselves. To involve youth in appropriate theater training, is to provide them with the power to tell others of their concerns, their frustrations, their pains, their dreams. Theater empowers youth to speak for themselves in a way that others will hear. It requires discipline and commitment, and in return it gives voice. All youth benefit from the kind of theatre training which requires that they speak their own thoughts within this discipline. The disenfranchised benefit particularly. African American youth, as a group, are disenfranchised. Theater and theater training for African American youth can be part of a program of enfranchisement. Inherent in the process must be an awareness of, a valuing of, an incorporation of the African American aesthetic. Theatre can be power.

Selected Bibliography

Bullins, Ed, ed. NEW PLAYS FROM THE BLACK THEATRE.
New York: Bantam Books, 1969.

Hatch, James. "A White Folks Guide to Two Hundred Years of Black and White Drama." THE DRAMA REVIEW 16(December 1972): 5-24.

Hughes, Langston. SELECTED POEMS (New York: Alfred Knopf, 1979).

Jeyifo, Abiodun. "Black Critics on Black Theatre in America." THE DRAMA REVIEW 18(September 1974): 34-45.

King, Woodie and Milner, Ron, eds. BLACK DRAMA ANTHOLOGY. New York: Signet Books, 1971.

Neal, Larry. "The Black Arts Movement." THE DRAMA REVIEW 12 (Summer 1968): 29-39.